Praise for *F*

Anyone could benefit from *F*
why. And how. She distills decades of research on the psychology and biology of human emotion and attachment. But
don't let that scare you. *Feeling Loved* is an engaging read. Dr.
Segal supports us without coddling us. She tells us exactly how
to become more open to ourselves and each other. If you follow her prescription, you will become more self-aware and less
self-conscious. You will also learn how to improve your chances
of living an engaged and satisfying life.
—MICHAEL CRAIG MILLER, MD,
Harvard Medical School

GOT STRESS? Feeling empty? This book is for YOU! This
book is an amazing gem! Dr. Segal takes us into the heart of
what makes our lives satisfying and gives us specific tools for
moving from our stressed-out, meaningless existence to the
capacity to actually FEEL loved. In these pages we are touched
by her own and others' stories that help us understand how we
got here. She takes us step by practical step and includes many
other free resources that help us maintain our newfound sense
of feeling loved.
—MARTI GLENN, PHD,
former Dean, Santa Barbara Graduate Institute

Hoping that we can change is one thing, but being given the
tools to actually change is the gift that Dr. Segal gives us.
Feeling Loved incorporates the most recent findings of brain
research and shows us the effect of stress on our lives and
what we can do to replace stress with love. Dr. Segal writes in
a warm, engaging manner and gives us a path and the skills

to achieve real change and attain the goal that so many of us harbor—to feel loved. This is one book I'll keep on my bedside table and continually refer to.

—MARGOT WINCHESTER,
documentary, film, and TV producer

Also by Jeanne Segal

The Language of Emotional
Intelligence: The Five Essential Tools
for Building Powerful and Effective Relationships

Raising Your Emotional
Intelligence: A Practical Guide

Living Beyond Fear: Coping with
the Emotional Aspects of Life-Threatening Illness

Feeling Great: A Personal Program
to Speed Healing and Enhance Wellness

FEELING
LOVED

FEELING LOVED

LOVED

The Science of Nurturing

Meaningful Connections and

Building Lasting Happiness

JEANNE SEGAL

BenBella

BenBella Books, Inc.

Dallas, Texas

The case studies in this book are composites from Dr. Segal's practice. All names and circumstances have been fictionalized to protect privacy. The ideas, practices, suggestions, and other material in this book are for informational purposes only and should not be used as a substitute for professional medical or mental health advice, diagnosis, or treatment.

BenBella Books, Inc.
10300 N. Central Expressway, Suite #530 | Dallas, TX 75231
www.benbellabooks.com | Send feedback to feedback@benbellabooks.com

Printed in the United States of America
10 9 8 7 6 5 4 3 2 1

Library of Congress Cataloging-in-Publication Data
Segal, Jeanne, 1939-
Feeling loved : the science of nurturing meaningful connections and building lasting happiness / by Jeanne Segal.
    pages cm
    ISBN 978-1-941631-47-8 (paperback) — ISBN 978-1-941631-99-7 (electronic) 1. Love. 2. Interpersonal relations. 3. Stress management. 4. Happiness. I. Title.
    BF575.L8S44 2015
    158.2—dc23
                    2015020259

Editing by Leah Wilson and Vy Tran | Copyediting by Stacia Seaman
Proofreading by Brittney Martinez and Kim Broderick
Text design and composition by Silver Feather Design
Front cover design by Vanessa No Heart
Full cover design by Sarah Dombrowsky
Printed by Lake Book Manufacturing

Distributed by Perseus Distribution | www.perseusdistribution.com
To place orders through Perseus Distribution:
Tel: (800) 343-4499 | Fax: (800) 351-5073
E-mail: orderentry@perseusbooks.com

Significant discounts for bulk sales are available. Please contact Glenn Yeffeth at glenn@benbellabooks.com or 214-750-3628.

*To Robert, whose endearing love makes
everything possible, and to Jeff and Viktoria.*

Contents

Introduction: Love Is an Experience Everyone Needs—and Can Have

Have you ever seen others giving and receiving love around you, feeling like you're on the outside looking in? Like staring at paradise behind a locked gate, you can see heaven yet feel as though it's out of reach. Similarly, there seems to be a barrier between you and the experience of love, and you long and ache for it. Here's a secret: You're not imagining it, and you are not alone. Science reveals that the desire to feel loved is real and universal—even if we can't always seem to get our arms around it. And though we may do things that interfere with our ability to feel loved, we're not hopeless. Research in brain science and early child development and new emotional inroads in psychology provide a road map for finding the answers we need.

In the 1990s, there was an explosion of brain research that overlapped with early child development and psychology. Researchers discovered that when an infant feels loved, he or she undergoes profoundly positive effects in brain development. These studies also support the idea that feeling loved has beneficial impacts on our physiology, making us more resilient and nourishing our nervous and immune systems so we can better face life's challenges. It doesn't come as a surprise, then, that much of the loneliness, sadness, anger, and anxiety we feel are reflections of the emptiness we experience when we *don't* feel loved. As such a powerful force, it's no wonder artists and poets, as well as scientists, have remained enthralled for thousands of years with the subject of attaining love.

The more we learn about the brain, the more we discover concrete evidence that demonstrates humans are profoundly social and emotional. We have a real need not only to feel the love others have for us but also to ensure that those we care about feel loved. Yet because many people struggle with giving and receiving love, it can feel like there's an enormous gap between what we need and what we know about getting it. In reality, the gap isn't as wide as it seems. That's because today we recognize that our brains can change, so we can develop new ways of thinking, feeling, and acting. We are able to make life-changing social and emotional changes.

Unfortunately, there are also obstacles that prevent us from doing so. We have stressful habits that stand in the way of our desire for change and leave us feeling empty. We have fast-paced lifestyles filled with technological distractions and oversimplified solutions to complex problems that keep us from what we really need. When I first began working with people as a therapist, the brain was mostly a mystery, so addressing these kinds of obstacles could be difficult. Now, with modern technology, our eyes have been opened to so much potential for using brain science to change or improve our habits, especially to the inherent power in feeling loved.

One of my first clients, however, was able to show me this power without any hard scientific evidence. Through a woman named Monica, I came face-to-face with a force that awakened me to the extraordinary influence that feeling loved can have on every aspect of our lives.

The woman who discovered nurturing love

Monica was a petite, vibrant woman in her mid-thirties who had lived with diabetes since childhood. She was a member of a diabetic support group I led. One day she asked to see me privately.

Monica was at a crossroads in a long-term relationship and wanted to explore her options. Having grown up under the protection of anxious parents who felt it was in their daughter's best interest for her to lead a very quiet, uneventful life, Monica didn't have much experience with relationships. Monica's boyfriend of more than five years was a nice person who didn't seem particularly interested in her, nor did he ask much of her, which made her question her feelings for him and the relationship overall. I encouraged Monica to be honest with her boyfriend and make herself available for new romantic possibilities.

Several weeks went by and I was beginning to wonder what happened to Monica when I received a shocking call from her doctor. He told me that Monica had collapsed and was in the hospital. Many of her organs were shutting down and she was not expected to live. The doctor asked me to visit and prepare Monica for the worst that might be ahead.

Because of my recent work with dying cancer patients, I was used to making near-death hospital visits. However, nothing I had experienced prepared me for this visit. When I walked into Monica's room I found her sitting up in bed attached to an IV, looking remarkably well for someone presumed to be dying. When she saw me, she put her finger to her lips and asked me to close the door.

"You'll never guess what happened," she said. "I found someone!"

I sat there with my eyes wide and jaw hanging as Monica told me she had broken up with her boyfriend and recently met a man named Phillip, who continued to see her in the hospital after her collapse. Phillip spent time listening to Monica, talking and laughing with her, asking her questions, and being engrossed in her answers. The best part about this new relationship was that neither the hospital nor her illness seemed to frighten or discourage Phillip. He had a dearly beloved sister who had been ill most of her life, so he was used to medical challenges. The more Monica and Phillip talked, the more engaged and excited she became. Monica then told me that two nights prior, she had bribed the night nurse and, still attached to her IV pole, she had taken the elevator down to the hospital garage where—as impossible as this may seem—Monica made passionate love for the first time in the backseat of Phillip's car.

I drove home that night feeling certain that Monica's life wasn't over yet—and I was proven right. She eventually left the hospital and some months later married

Phillip. I never saw her again, but I followed her for years through the postcards she sent telling me how she was doing. Monica and Phillip bought a small home near the canals in Venice, California, and traveled a great deal. They even took vacations in developing countries, which surprised me given her medical history. Yes, she did get sick again, but each time she would recover, determined to embrace the life she found fulfilling. Monica's serious health challenges proved less influential on her well-being than the nurturing, motivating love she experienced and gave.

Monica is an example of how someone's life can change by feeling loved. Her life didn't just change, though; she was saved. In a setting that didn't allow them to do much more than communicate with one another, Phillip demonstrated a keen interest in thoroughly getting to know Monica. He wanted to understand what she felt, as well as what she thought, and his approving interest and encouragement made her feel deeply known and valued. For the first time, Monica knew what it was to feel loved.

Monica's experience made me look closer at the different kinds of problems men and women have brought to my office. Over the years I saw individuals, couples, and families from many ethnic and socioeconomic backgrounds present with a wide range of problems—they were depressed, anxious, unproductive, unhappy, sick, and sick at heart. Their problems varied, but all had two things in common: They were intensely stressed, and none of them felt loved.

Sometimes a spouse or family member felt an absence of love from a loved one who insisted this was not true. Sometimes I could understand why they felt unloved, but not always. At times the feelings of those who felt unloved seemed rooted in an inability to feel *anything*, good or bad. Many of these people seemed completely preoccupied with thoughts about something that had happened, might happen, or could happen. So absorbed were they in their thoughts that they were missing their experience in the moment.

DISCOVERING THE ROLE EMOTIONAL AWARENESS AND CONNECTION PLAYS IN OUR LIVES

As I was completing my doctorate, I had an opportunity to become part of an experimental program with end-of-life cancer patients at UCLA. The program focused on something new at the time called "holistic health," which brought a wider view to health issues. The opportunity was a good fit for me. My husband, Robert, and I began exploring the subject of holistic health in a series of very popular conferences we coordinated for the Association for Humanistic Psychology.

This broader view of health that I embraced affected the direction of my work. The interventions I participated in included many new theories and therapies developed in the sixties and seventies. It was heady stuff, especially when we saw that some of the men and women we worked with weren't dying but had been, in fact, surviving for more than seven years. Because of this, I was assigned a research project that sought to discover a connection between our interventions and the survival rate of our patients.

After years of false starts and dead ends, we finally found a link between the relationship our patients had with their emotions and stress—and their ability to survive. Those who recognized what they felt, accepted all their feelings, and used their emotional awareness in their decision-making processes appeared to make better decisions and have a better chance of survival than those who did not. Though we had no idea why this might be true, I learned that emotions *matter* and that stress plays a role in blunting emotional awareness.

SEARCHING FOR ANSWERS TO QUESTIONS ABOUT EMOTIONAL CONNECTION

With the aim of reducing stress and increasing emotional awareness for patients, I began developing a prototype for a meditation that could teach people how to remain aware and comfortable with their emotional experience—even when that experience is unpleasant. My understanding of the role emotions play in preserving someone's well-being led to the publication of my second book, *Living Beyond Fear*.

In the 1980s, as the pharmaceutical industry began to dominate the mental health field, my interest in practicing therapy waned. I believed that emotion-altering drugs had their place in someone's recovery, but they were not producing long-term solutions for most mental health problems. Then, in the nineties, there was an explosion in brain research and technology. When I saw the connection between what I knew about emotions and the new field of emotional intelligence, I began to deeply explore the subject. My findings led me to write two books on emotional intelligence and its connection to emotional awareness.

As the millennium approached, I became increasingly interested in how emotional health, or its absence, first develops. I coordinated two community conferences in Los Angeles titled "From Neurons to Neighborhoods," which brought together leaders in the field to discuss this subject. It gave both the public and industry professionals the opportunity to learn about the newest advances in the understanding of brain development, stress, and trauma.

As I absorbed all this information, I was learning more about the role emotions and intense levels of stress play in our mental health problems. I was also learning more about the brain's ability to change itself and our ability to intervene in this change. As I observed, worked with, and labored to help others, I also made personal discoveries that have changed me to a degree I never believed possible.

REFLECTIONS ON MY PERSONAL JOURNEY

My parents were good people, and today I have no doubt that they loved me. Yet, as a child, I felt unloved. Both of my parents were hardworking and devoted to my well-being; they did their best for my sister and me, yet neither of us felt we got the love we needed. I survived by withdrawing from my emotions and becoming an observer of things. I paid attention to other people and to nature, and when I felt lonely, I comforted myself by taking out my crayons and drawing for long periods of time.

If I was a somewhat lonely and isolated child, I was even more so as a teenager. I was popular with my teachers but unpopular with classmates. I was shy, but when something seemed hurtful or wrong, I became energized and let my feelings be known. Because I was attractive and a serious student, I received attention from different people, but the attention never felt meaningful. There were some unknowns that I longed for and tried to find in books. I looked for something that would make me feel safe and whole, but I didn't know what it was and had absolutely no idea of how to get it. So I kept searching.

Fortunately, I had the opportunity to thoroughly indulge my curiosities in many things. It began with an interest in art and the liberal arts; then I became engrossed in the psyche, psychology, and the relationship we have with ourselves. In college, when I found the self too narrow a subject, I switched my major to sociology. I soon led women's groups and trained as a marriage and family counselor and as a social worker.

I faced the biggest challenge to my own mental health during the brain research and technology boom of the nineties. In 1996, our adored daughter Morgan Leslie lost her battle with depression worsened by a variety of antidepressants and other medications, and took her own life. This tested everything I believed in and everything I had ever written. I only survived by fully embracing the feelings of grief that defined my day-to-day existence for the next four years. At one point, I said to myself, "If this is the way I'm going to feel for the rest of my life, so be it." The experience has left me stronger, wiser, and more determined than ever to fully embrace life. Our daughter's death also made me recognize the gap that can exist between being loved and *feeling* loved. Morgan Leslie was deeply loved by her family and by all who knew her, but I don't believe she felt loved.

As a way of preserving our daughter's memory, my husband, Robert, and I created a nonprofit mental health website. Helpguide.org was launched in 1999, inspired by our belief that Morgan Leslie's tragedy could have been avoided if she had access to unbiased, reliable information that gave her a sense of hope and direction. Since then, the website has grown from a small project in Santa Monica, California, to an internationally recognized resource serving over 65 million visitors a year. As Helpguide.org has grown, so has my understanding of the challenges people all over the world wake up to every day. Rooted in most of these challenges is the profound need to feel loved and to make those we care about feel loved.

Feeling Loved: The Science of Nurturing Meaningful Connections and Building Lasting Happiness is dedicated to helping those who don't feel loved. My goal is for you to experience this feeling, and to share it with others.

This is a multilayered book, rooted in half a dozen sciences, that draws a distinction between being loved and feeling loved. In addition to providing the reader with tools for recognizing this distinction, this book also examines why many of us are missing something as important as the experience of feeling loved.

This book was also written to spur you into action. It's important that you put yourself in motion. But before you do so, you need to understand not only what you're looking for and why, but also what habits and assumptions stand in your way. Change for the better happens in the context of replacing old ways of being with new, more productive experiences. This book is a road map that begins by explaining why the experience of feeling loved is essential for health and happiness. It also offers tools and other resources for attaining this end, but between the explanation and the effort to provide solutions is a section that addresses common obstacles that slow or block intentions for change. Sometimes the main reason for not doing what we want to do is that we are too busy doing something else.

Part One of *Feeling Loved* explains why the experience we have when we feel ourselves loved is essential for health and happiness. Part Two describes the habits and assumptions that may interfere with this intention. Part Three provides tools and other resources for making the experience of feeling loved an ongoing part of your life; and Part Four gives you a snapshot of what these skills look like in action.

There is also a connection between the advertisement-free, nonprofit Helpguide.org website and this book. My intention in linking *Feeling Loved* to the website is two-fold: first, to provide an additional source of inspiration and information for overcoming challenges and improving lives; and second, to offer online a free, complete, step-by-step program with audio and video supports.

As a final note, this book has been written for a lay audience, but it is based on decades of research, a portion of which is listed in the bibliography.

—JEANNE SEGAL, PHD

PART I

FULL LIVES

AND EMPTY HEARTS

We have more things than ever before: more possessions, more food, more contacts, and more access to information and places around the world. Our lives, with our smart devices and the Internet, have never been fuller. But even though we appear full and plugged into the world around us, we are less and less plugged into our feelings and emotions, and more and more stressed. Our connections to our personal relationships and ourselves have been pulled from the wall, leaving us with empty hearts and, most importantly, a sense of not feeling loved. But we are not victims of a dilemma we can't control or do anything about. Feeling loved—once we understand what it is and how we limit ourselves from having this experience—is an attainable goal for everyone willing to learn new skills.

CHAPTER 1

The Experience
of Feeling Loved

LOVE AND FEAR ARE THE TWO most important emotional influences in our lives. One or the other motivates much of what we feel, think, and do every day. Both produce reflexive biological responses. When we're frightened, a cascade of hormones automatically causes us to get angry, flee, or freeze. When we feel loved, other hormones are triggered that make us feel safe, secure, and happy. Feeling loved causes us to overflow with joyous feelings, and because we feel protected, our hearts and our minds are receptive and open. Fear, on the other hand, shuts us down, stripping our lives of positive feelings, stressing our bodies, and narrowing our minds.

With the ability to make ourselves happy, calm, focused, and relaxed, the state of being we achieve when we feel loved is unlike any other. Feeling loved is such a powerful experience that it can ward off stressors and support resilience in the face of challenges. Feeling loved isn't a "take it or leave it" choice; it's a biological need like water or food, something that we long for when it's not part of our experience. When we don't feel loved, we instinctively know that something important is missing in our lives.

So many of us today feel isolated and alone—evidence that fear is gaining control over our lives. Though we have more technology, entertainment, and opportunities to connect with others than ever before, we feel that our lives are shrinking rather than expanding. As individuals, and as a society, we are growing increasingly troubled. More than half of those who marry end up divorced—often more than once. Half of us live alone, often not by choice, and one in four Americans say they have no one to confide in. The loneliness, sense of alienation, and emotional distress we feel highlights that we don't feel loved. Our efforts to feel loved, and to make others feel loved, have been negated by interests and habits that not only dull our fears but also block our ability to get the kind of love we want and need.

Feeling loved depends on our ability to communicate emotionally. We can learn skills that foster this ability that when put into practice reward us with the opportunity to feel loved both now and for the rest of our lives. The first step is to understand what we experience when we feel loved, and why it's so difficult to identify and value this feeling.

WE NEED LOVE BUT
DON'T KNOW HOW TO GET IT

We all want love in our lives, but often we don't know how to find or keep it. One of the reasons for this is that while we know we want it, we don't know enough about what love really feels like. We don't know what it takes to make us feel loved or what it takes to make those we care about feel loved. We don't understand why we make such poor choices at times, or why we can't seem to make good choices. We certainly don't see the things we do that sabotage our ability to love and feel loved. In the stories below, Libby, Oscar, and Karen are examples of people who long to feel loved but don't know what to look for—or are too afraid to let themselves be loved.

The woman who didn't see love

Libby grew up in the middle of a large family that had little interest in her apart from the fact that she was an exceptionally pretty child. By the time she was a toddler, Libby had given up trying to get noticed by any means other than smiling, batting her eyes, and acting coy. The habit was so ingrained in her that when she became an adult, she acted the same way with men. A man named Peter, though, saw more in Libby than just a pretty girl, and after a short courtship, they were married. It never occurred to Libby that Peter actually cared about how she felt about herself and the world around her, and not just about the way she looked. She continued to focus on outward appearances, all the while doing her best to be a good wife and mother who paid attention to the physical needs of her family. But because she didn't look for emotional connections, no one in the family got the love they needed, and her relationship with Peter and her children suffered.

The man whose fear kept him from experiencing love

Oscar grew up being cared for by a series of nannies—a rather long series. As a result, he became a tense, vigilant child who feared intimacy, focusing on elaborate gadgetry rather than people. He was intelligent but insecure and distrustful, believing that because he came from a wealthy family, people only liked him for his money. In his thirties, he traveled all over the world visiting religious sites, always searching for a greater sense of security and peace of mind.

Oscar's first wife was his social equal, but that marriage ended in divorce, leaving him even more fearful of intimacy. Then on a charity mission to help less fortunate children, he met Francis, a woman who recognized Oscar's emotional problems but also saw the kindness and goodness in him. For the first time in his life, Oscar experienced being loved and believed that someone loved him. In the beginning, they were happy traveling and exploring the world together, but soon Oscar's old insecurities began to take hold. Fearing that Francis only married him for his money, he ignored Francis's care and concern and distanced himself from her physical warmth. Francis tried in vain for many years to make Oscar feel loved, but he remained unavailable, and eventually she gave up trying, and they divorced.

The woman who didn't recognize love

Because her mother was an alcoholic, **Karen** had a childhood that was confusing and traumatic. There were times when her mother was loving and tender, but there were other times when she screamed and called Karen stupid and worthless. Until the day Karen graduated from high school and left home, her stepfather did his best to protect Karen from her mother, but the damage was too deep. Not surprisingly, Karen lacked self-confidence in the real world. She compensated by being clever and exceptionally hardworking.

Her first job was as a filing clerk, but her eagerness to prove herself helped her advance to a managerial position within a year. For the first time in her life, Karen began to relax and let down her guard. Many of the men at the company were interested in dating Karen, but she kept her distance until she met Tony. Tony swept Karen off her feet with his self-confidence, charm, and good looks, but since she had so little experience of being in a loving relationship, Karen failed to notice how much Tony's behavior resembled her mother's. After a few drinks, Tony, like her mother, became mean and nasty, but it wasn't until after she married Tony that Karen realized the truth.

People like Libby, Oscar, and Karen long to feel loved, but because they don't know what to look for or are too fearful to look at all, they miss the opportunities right in front of them. Some of us can identify with stories like those of Libby, Oscar, or Karen, but not all of us see the role we play in our failed efforts to experience emotional fulfillment. What we do tend to recognize is that *more* increasingly feels like *less*.

WHY MORE FEELS LIKE LESS

More can feel like less when we're not getting what we need. When we're absorbed in the pursuit of things we want, to the exclusion of things we need to feel and be our best, it's possible to be both full and empty at the same time.

Just as you can eat without being nourished and drink without quenching your thirst, you can technically *be* connected without *feeling* connected. You can have hundreds of friends online, but if you're not making connections that make you feel secure and valued, then it's nearly impossible to feel fulfilled. You can also care for others—and receive care yourself—without giving or getting the experience of being valued that you need.

SIGNS THAT WE'RE NOT FEELING LOVED

It's difficult to put feelings into words, especially feelings of emptiness or longing. But what we're missing might be revealed by answers to specific questions. Do you have someone you could contact in the middle of the night if you're upset, someone who would not only listen to you but also would genuinely care about what you're feeling and want to help? Would your spouse or partner want to talk to you, or would he or she just roll over and tell you to go back to sleep? Or if you live alone, do you have someone who would be there to console you when you're down and celebrate with you when you're excited? Do you have someone you trust and feel safe with? Are you sure that the people you love actually *feel* loved by you? Do they know that you appreciate them as they really are? If the answer to any of these questions is "no," you or those you care about may be missing the experience of *feeling* loved.

BEING LOVED DIFFERS FROM FEELING LOVED

Being loved is not the same as feeling loved. There is a difference between being taken care of and feeling cared for. You can tend to someone and provide and care for them, but if you don't slow down enough or know how to create an emotional connection, you won't experience feeling loved. Someone can go out of their way to meet your every physical and intellectual need, yet completely miss opportunities to notice and respond to your *emotional* needs. If they don't look at you, they may miss the fact that you're feeling sad. If they don't hear the frustration or fear in your voice, they may respond in ways that make you angrier or more fearful. When this happens, you realize that you're well cared for, but you don't feel loved. Without the facial, body language, and other nonverbal signals that convey emotional understanding and connection, you won't feel loved and be emotionally fulfilled—and many scientific discoveries explain why.

THE SCIENCE BEHIND THE NEED TO EXPERIENCE POSITIVE EMOTIONAL CONNECTION

Love has interested artists, poets, and musicians for centuries, but not until recently has the experience of feeling loved captured the attention of scientists. A wide number of scientific disciplines are now focusing on subjects that explain why—in order to be both healthy and happy—we need to feel emotionally connected to others in ways that make us feel loved. Such varied disciplines as biochemistry, neuroscience, early child development, psychology, mental health, and mind-brain study have discovered why positive emotional connection to others is so important both physically and emotionally.

Feeling loved: A focus of neuroscience and early child development

The focus brain science gives a newborn's experience of feeling loved has sparked an entirely new field of study: the study of infant development. In the 1990s brain research and technology uncovered the startling fact that at birth the connections between cells in the human brain, unlike all other organs in the body, are largely disorganized. No less surprising or important is the fact that the brain's organization reflects the experience infants and young children have with their mothers or other primary caretakers. The human brain is thus profoundly dependent on social connections and remains attuned to nonverbal, emotional social cues throughout life.

Brain science also shows that, unlike other organs in the body, the brain can produce new cells and connections to other cells throughout life. This characteristic of the brain gives us the opportunity to build healthy new neural structures even as the old brain structure remains imperfect or even diseased.

The knowledge that positive brain change is possible throughout life makes the study of early childhood development especially relevant to us as adults. Research from all corners of the globe tells us that humans come into this world needing a special kind of relationship in order to feel safe, thrive, and be happy. This secure relationship is one characterized by a nonverbal, emotional exchange between caretaker and infant that makes the infant feel seen, understood, and valued. In fact, a recent but widely accepted theory by Dr. Stephen Porges, former director of the Brain-Body Center at the University of Illinois at Chicago, has shed light on why we need this shared, nonverbal, emotional experience not only at birth, but consistently throughout our lives.

Feeling loved is nature's antidote to stress

Based on his research, Porges redefines the functions of the autonomic nervous system and the role played by the vagus (or tenth cranial) nerve. He describes the parasympathetic branch of the nervous system and the vagal nerve as having not one but two distinct pathways. The primitive reptilian pathway produces the freeze or immobility response, which we have recognized for some time. In addition, Porges has identified a second pathway. This second pathway, found only in mammals, produces a very different and much more social response when faced with situations that are perceived as threatening.

Porges names the second vagal pathway *the social engagement pathway* because it connects to the face, including the eyes, mouth, and middle ear. This pathway seeks and picks up wordless expressions and sounds from those nearby that communicate safety and provide comfort. This pathway also connects to the heart's cardiovascular system and to the emotional parts of the brain. Its function is to regulate stress, but it does so by putting the brakes on the older nervous system's strategies for protection. When this more social pathway experiences a threat, it can spring into action, overriding the more primitive responses. When the sympathetic branch receives signals of safety and recognition, fight and flight messages are suspended. In humans, the primitive pathways are activated only when the social engagement pathway fails. By avoiding the older responses, our minds remain clear and our emotions are kept on track.

Polyvagal theory makes it clear why it is so important to feel loved—not only in infancy but throughout life. In order to control stress and keep our thinking and emotions on track, we need experiences that make us feel loved. When we are threatened, exhausted, or overwhelmed, feeling loved can make us feel whole and relaxed. Aided by emotional cues that are seen, heard, and felt in the heart, nonverbal exchanges neutralize stress. Painful feelings can be replaced by sensations that return us to a relaxed state. In a flash, we can go from feeling stirred up to feeling relaxed. Feeling loved is nature's antidote for stress.

Positive psychology makes a strong case for feeling loved

The study of positive psychology, which is about what *really* makes people happy, finds that most of the things we think will make us happy—don't! Many people tell themselves, "I can't be happy until I find the right job, get rich, have a good relationship, marry the right person, have kids." They also tell themselves that they can't be happy because their dream didn't come true or because they're too old or too sick.

None of the research in positive psychology supports the notion that lasting happiness has to do with any of the above. What has proven to be true is that what makes people happy—not only in the moment or for only a short period of time—is their pleasurable involvement with others. Even when we think this isn't the case, *it is*. For example: When people are asked if they would rather sit alone when traveling or talk to someone seated next to them, they say they would rather be by themselves. But in experiments carried out to test this assumption, those who sat next to others reported that they found the trip far more enjoyable than those who sat alone. Even when we think we don't need others, we do.

Both happiness and its lasting effect may relate to the relief of stress that we can experience in the company of others or the fact that engaged conversation usually keeps us focused in the moment. But more than the absence of stress or avoiding the possibility of overthinking, positive social contexts provide opportunities for engagement, laughter, playfulness, and other positive emotional experiences.

EMOTIONAL INTELLIGENCE IS A FIELD THAT UNDERSCORES THE VALUE OF FEELING LOVED

The study of emotional intelligence, whether defined as a separate form of intelligence or not, clearly adds value to our work and professional lives by improving intuition, creativity, and performance. It isn't surprising that those who function well working with others and who inspire others to do their best work are people who experience positive emotions and know how to make others feel loved. Because of their ability to connect emotionally with themselves and others, they are able to manage their own stress and relationship stress. This, in turn, encourages them and those they work with to remain calm, think clearly, be creative, and act productively.

Emotional intelligence underscores the value of emotional awareness and emotional management, giving us a wider range of information and experience from which to problem solve and make informed decisions. There is no arguing the fact that positive emotional connections at work result in less stress and greater work satisfaction, happiness, and productivity.

The biochemistry of feeling loved

In general, when we're on to something, when something is important, its truth shows up in a number of different disciplines, as is the case with the experience of feeling loved. Not only are neuroscientists, social scientists, and psychologists discovering its value, so have chemists.

For more than a hundred years neuroscientists have been investigating the experience of feeling loved from a biochemical perspective. What they have discovered is that the hormone oxytocin facilitates loving experiences and social behavior. Oxytocin's role in endocrine function begins before pregnancy, continues during birth, and remains a lasting part of our lives. The hormone travels from the brain to the heart and throughout the entire body, reducing stress and triggering emotions that include attraction, affection, and happiness.

Oxytocin, known as the bonding or love hormone, counteracts stress hormones such as cortisol that can exhaust our adrenal glands and damage, sometimes severely, our bodies and brains. Oxytocin receptors are involved in many social and emotional behaviors, and the hormone is responsible for strong connections not only with our children but also with our partners, friends, and even pets.

Oxytocin is triggered by the exchange of nonverbal emotional cues that express attention, understanding, approval, and affection. Such cues include hugs, kisses, holding hands, gazing into someone's eyes, and other positive nonverbal cues. Infants only a few weeks old can make eye contact, mirror gestures, and participate in mutual exchanges of these cues with smiles and sounds of pleasure. Throughout our lives oxytocin enriches the pleasure, happiness, and joy we experience when we feel loved.

IN ORDER TO FEEL LOVED, WE NEED TO SLOW OUR PACE

Emotional communication on the run is rarely successful. In order to be aware of what we are feeling and what others are feeling, we need to slow down. The feeling of being loved and the biological response it stimulates is triggered by nonverbal cues: the tone in a voice, the expression on a face, or the touch that feels just right. Nonverbal cues—rather than spoken words—make us feel that the person we are with is interested in, understands, and values us. When we're with them, we feel safe. We even see the power of nonverbal cues in the wild. After evading the chase of predators, animals often nuzzle each other as a means of stress relief. This bodily contact provides reassurance of safety and relieves stress.

Yes, words have meaning, especially when exchanged with someone you love. But the impact words have depends on the success or failure of what is *not said*—the wordless exchanges. If there is an inconsistency between *what* is being said and *how* it is being said, we feel it instantly and become confused or skeptical. If the words and body language someone uses don't match up, then we won't feel loved.

In order to effectively pick up nonverbal cues, we need to pause and focus on what's happening from one moment to the next. Nonverbal cues often come and go rapidly, so it's important to pay close attention. When we get too busy or too preoccupied to accommodate the slower pace required for emotional communication, we lose the hormonal rush that makes us feel loved. If we are always on the go, planning the next step, multitasking, or just too exhausted to notice, we will miss opportunities to feel loved or to make others feel loved, as the following story illustrates.

The loving couple that didn't know what they needed to feel loved

Maribel couldn't believe her luck when she met Ben. Like her, he was from an immigrant family, worked hard, and enjoyed the outdoors. Soon, they fell in love and were married. They decided together to focus on building Ben's career as a lawyer, and the next couple of years were hectic and a bit lonely as Ben put in long hours at the office. But they were happy. Maribel watched every penny and postponed having the family she wanted. Ben felt very supported and appreciated Maribel's sacrifices, but their feelings of closeness began fading as Ben threw himself into his growing law practice.

As Ben's firm took off and he made more money, Maribel saw less and less of her husband. When they did talk, he seemed preoccupied, rarely looking at her. Ben was always on the go, busy multitasking, with his mind and attention someplace else. Everything revolved around Ben's work, even their social life. A year later, the couple had a baby boy and Maribel occupied herself by taking care of their son and a new house. It was around this time Maribel started feeling anxious. She knew something was wrong, that something was missing, but she didn't know what it was. Her husband treated her well, giving her elaborate gifts and providing for her and their family. Nevertheless, Maribel found herself growing increasingly worried about many things that never bothered her in the past. She felt as though she were losing her zest for life. When she mentioned these feelings to her doctor, he prescribed anti-anxiety medication, which eased her worrying but also numbed the pleasure she took in doing things she normally enjoyed. A couple of months later, she began to put on weight and stopped taking the medication.

Life went on, and Ben was sympathetic, but Maribel sensed that her inability to relax and enjoy herself was becoming a burden to him, as well as to herself. Then something happened that brought their lives to a standstill: Ben was diagnosed with cancer.

Because the oncology office offered free counseling to patients and their families, Maribel—sensing that for Ben's sake she had to do something about her anxiety—made an appointment. With a little encouragement, Maribel described her life and marriage. When asked why she hadn't shared her feelings of loneliness and anxiety with her husband, she said she was afraid of burdening Ben with her feelings, especially now that he was sick.

It hadn't occurred to Mirabel that Ben, too, might miss the connection they once had. In the context of having more time to spend together—even if it was time spent talking face-to-face while Ben got his chemotherapy—Maribel described her sadness and longing for the emotional intimacy they used to share. With no time pressure or work agenda, Ben relaxed, and with tears in his eyes admitted that he, too, missed the tenderness they had once shared.

Ben's recovery became an opportunity to renew their relationship. When Ben went back to the work he loved, he made sure to carve out time exclusively for the two of them; they had leisurely morning coffee dates and evening walks, and started traveling. By once more sharing emotional as well as physical intimacy, both of them felt loved. Ben recovered from his cancer, and Maribel's anxiety became a background issue in lives that now felt emotionally fulfilling.

FEELING LOVED HAPPENS IN THE MOMENT AND FACE-TO-FACE

Feeling loved is an experience that goes beyond "thought-to-action." It happens face-to-face, from one moment to the next, between you and another person. The way you look, listen, move, and react to another person tells them more about how you're feeling—and how you're feeling about them—than words alone ever can. Bonnie's story below is an example of using nonverbal cues to make others feel loved.

The teacher who made her students feel loved

Bonnie entered a Catholic order of teachers at eighteen and was immediately thrown into a classroom of forty-five first graders in an inner-city neighborhood. Without much instruction, she was expected to teach reading and writing. Bonnie was nervous, but to her amazement—and the amazement of her Mother Superior—she was an exceptional teacher who seemed to love every minute in the classroom. Bonnie soon became the envy of all the other teachers. How was she able to get forty-five squirming little bodies to hold still and pay attention long enough to learn? How did someone so young and inexperienced manage to not only control but also captivate such a large group of first graders?

Any time Bonnie attended to a child's question or need, she did so with a sincere sense of interest and wonderment. Also, she was never critical, judgmental, or blaming; Bonnie felt that each child deserved her reverent, undivided attention. Soon, every child in the class wanted to experience her rapt attention, and by the end of the day, they all did.

Bonnie also spoke quietly. She never raised her voice; instead, she made sure that her words were expressive and laden with emotion. The children in the back of the room sometimes had to work hard to hear their teacher, but the effort was always worth it. And on the rare occasion the class got noisy or unruly, Bonnie grew quiet, putting her hands together near her chin and cocking her head a little, giving the impression that she was listening intently to all of them. Soon, the children who were speaking or being unruly got the point that Bonnie heard everything they were saying and they calmed down. What Bonnie's students experienced were feelings of recognition and understanding. In other words, they were eager learners because they felt loved.

When I was a young woman, I met psychologist Carl Rogers and psychiatrist Elisabeth Kübler-Ross, renowned healers who had the same effect on me that Bonnie had on her students. Carl and Elisabeth took the time to look at everyone they met with a focused interest and emotional intensity that made people feel relaxed and appreciated. It was as if they not only could see right through me but also *liked* what they saw. When I spoke to Carl, I remember being amused by the fact that I—a tall, strong, vigorous young woman—felt like crawling into the lap of this frail little man and laying my head on his shoulder. Of course, I didn't do that, but he made me feel so safe, and his presence was so comforting, it made me feel loved.

WHEN WE DON'T FEEL LOVED, IT'S HARD TO MAKE OTHERS FEEL LOVED

Bonnie, in the earlier story, found it easy to make others feel loved. Everyone she came into contact with felt special and important. People like Bonnie are the lucky ones who have experienced love and know how to pass it on. But not everyone is this fortunate. Many men and women don't know what it is to feel loved, and because of this, they have great difficulty making others feel loved. This was the case with Marsha.

The woman who didn't know how to make those she loved feel loved

Marsha felt unloved by her self-centered mother and grew up feeling depressed. She also grew up determined that her own children were not going to have the same experience; her children were going to get everything they needed to feel loved.

In her twenties, Marsha fell in love and married, and when it was time to start a family, she did everything she could think of to ensure that her children felt loved. She had natural childbirths, breast-fed her children, created fun-filled family vacations, and read countless parenting books on how to best raise healthy, happy, and smart kids. But because Marsha herself remained depressed from the experiences of her unloved childhood, she wasn't very aware of her own emotions or those of her children. Though she thought a great deal about her kids, she missed the red flags that her children didn't feel securely loved, lacked self-confidence, and felt insecure with peers in spite of the fact that each was deeply loved.

Marsha wrote off her children's behavior as "teenage angst," including her son's edginess, lack of friends, and unhealthy preoccupation with video games. When Marsha's daughter was younger, she was a dancer who had a lot of friends and talked incessantly about them. But as she grew older, she became quiet and reclusive, locking herself in her room every evening. Neither of her children had ever been willing to talk to Marsha about how they were feeling. Since Marsha rarely paid attention or understood what she was feeling herself, this all seemed normal.

Many years passed and Marsha's son found love in the wrong places, marrying and divorcing two women who were both steeped in their own problems. He struggled with anger issues and had few close friends. Marsha's daughter stopped dancing, gained a lot of weight, became chronically depressed, and rarely contacted her family. One night, alone in front of the television, Marsha finally realized that her children, despite her earlier promises, had grown up feeling unloved and insecure.

No matter how hard we try to make those we love feel loved, if we don't feel emotionally connected to ourselves, we won't be able to emotionally connect with them. And without this emotional connection, we won't be able to communicate nonverbally and tap the hormonal resources that bring so much pleasure and strength to our lives. Be reassured it's never too late to connect to your emotions and experience feelings of love.

IT'S NEVER TOO LATE TO BEGIN FEELING LOVED

We are never too old to feel loved. We are never too old to fall in love. As long as we are in good health, oxytocin can be triggered by vivid memories of loving and feeling loved and by being with people who make us feel loved. Let me tell you the story of Sarah and Sam.

The couple who took their time to fall in love

Sarah and **Sam** were both in their mid-seventies when they met and fell in love. Each had children and grandchildren, and each had been in a long marriage with a spouse who died. Though their spouses had been good people who cared for them, neither had felt loved or been in a passionate relationship. Since meeting each other, for the first time in their long lives both experienced a relationship with someone who looked directly at them, listened attentively when they spoke, cared about and understood what they felt, and brought emotion into their lovemaking. The couple's intention to wed shocked their children, but Sarah and Sam stood firm. They resolved to spend as much time together as they could—for as long as they lived—and married in spite of the opposition. Both Sarah and Sam's families eventually became grateful that they met, because each of them remained so healthy, busy, and happy that their children found no need to worry about them.

WE CAN LEARN NEW SKILLS IN ORDER TO LOVE AND FEEL LOVED

No matter our age, we can access tools and learn skills that enable us to feel loved and make others feel loved.

As far as we know, we are not simply born with an innate ability to produce an emotional connection. Emotional connection is a skill set that, if we're lucky, we learn early in life. But we don't have to acquire this skill set in infancy; we can learn these skills later in life. Even if you don't feel loved now—or if you've never felt loved—you can learn skills that will enable you to feel safe enough to connect deeply and emotionally with yourself and others, release oxytocin, and experience the feeling of love you need to overcome stress, thrive, and find happiness.

CHAPTER 2

Beating Stress
with Emotional Connection

THIS MAY SURPRISE YOU, BUT OUR emotions are responsible for many of the most important things we know and value about ourselves: Our motivation, action, judgment, personality, empathy, and love are all shaped by what we feel rather than what we think. Descartes said, "I think, therefore I am," but, "*I feel, therefore I am*," is closer to the truth.

As babies, we enter this world expressing our physical and emotional feelings in nonverbal ways that set the stage for intimate communication throughout our lives. Our first conversations are wordless and based on emotional cues. We feel hungry and anxiously look up at a person who conveys understanding and caring and offers us food. Emotionally reassured by what's been communicated, we relax even before we start feeding, feeling safe and content and connected.

When we feel loved, these feelings of safety and intimacy grow and deepen throughout our lives. As an adult in a relationship with someone who makes us feel loved, the reassuring scent of our partner nearby can immediately make us feel safe and help us fall peacefully back to sleep when we wake up scared from a nightmare. Likewise, if we get terrible news and feel as though we're about to spiral out of control, a familiar voice, a pair of caring eyes, or a reassuring embrace can ease our anxiety and override stress.

It's important to recognize that these feelings of safety that make us feel loved come in a package of feelings—we can't just have the emotions we enjoy experiencing unless we are also willing to have emotions we don't enjoy. This is why it's vital to remain connected to what we feel from moment to moment, not to pick and choose which emotions to feel, according to our likes or dislikes. Our emotions—including the unpleasant ones—are the lifelines of connection that keep us afloat. As Larry's story illustrates, when we disconnect from our emotions, we lose connection not only with ourselves but also with those we love.

The man who had an on/off relationship with his emotions

Larry had many friends and admirers, and for good reason. He was warm, funny, kind, and caring. He was also smart—often making brilliant decisions when it came to problems both at work and at home. But he wasn't like this all of the time. When Larry's stress was within a normal range, he was at the top of his game. However, when he became overwhelmed by stress and felt threatened, his judgment was impaired and he made foolish, inappropriate decisions. He tried to quash these threatening feelings by tightening his stomach, holding his breath, and gritting his teeth. His face would get red and he would yell and lash out angrily, stomping out of a room and slamming the door. This scared his young children, and he left his wife and associates shocked, confused, and hurt. Later, when he was in control again, he very much regretted his behavior.

Larry wasn't aware of it, but the more he tried to avoid his uncomfortable emotions, the more agitated and uncontrolled he became. When his stress was imbalanced, an automatic survival response was triggered that shut down his capacity to reason, greatly restricting his behavioral choices. Larry felt ashamed when he lost control, always promising himself and others that he would act differently in the future. In spite of his regrets and good intentions, however, nothing changed. If anything, the hair triggers that turned him from a high-functioning Dr. Jekyll to a frightening and confusing Mr. Hyde went off more and more as his regrets piled up.

Larry's family and friends are always on guard, never knowing what he, who is caring one minute and threatening the next, will do in any given moment. Larry's loved ones can never fully relax and feel safe around him. He loves his family and cares for his business partners, but because of his actions, they don't feel loved or cared for. Instead, they feel anxious, even when Larry is in a good mood. So not only do the people Larry loves feel unloved, but his responses also interfere with his ability to feel loved himself. If Larry could stay connected to the

> emotions he tries to avoid, he would discover a lot more
> self-control and the ability to feel and give more love.

EMOTIONS COME IN A MIXED BAG

Every emotion has a purpose. Core emotions like anger, sadness, or fear—though we don't welcome them—provide information to our brains that allows us to focus on choices that can protect our health and well-being. Anger generates a lot of energy and can be used in life-threatening situations by mobilizing us to action, often inspiring determination and creativity. Sadness asks us to slow down, open up, trust, and allow ourselves to be vulnerable in order to learn, heal, and recover from loss. Fear signals danger, triggering automatic life-saving reactions that protect us from harm.

Emotion has everything to do with helping us remain safe. But if we blunt or restrain our emotions or avoid emotions we dislike, we obstruct their purpose. When we diminish any emotion, we reduce the intensity of *all* our emotions—including those we want to experience.

EVEN THE MOST
PAINFUL EMOTIONS HAVE A PURPOSE

Most of the negativity we associate with feelings we dislike stems from our exhausting and futile attempts to avoid them, as Christine's story demonstrates.

The woman who survived by feeling her pain

Christine was a fine therapist who experienced her own emotions and the emotions of others. But nothing prepared her for the grief she felt when—after trying to become pregnant for several years—her daughter was stillborn.

Christine's grief was palpable; it was a deep and searing wound that she experienced throughout the day. The pain she felt was the last thing she remembered before falling asleep at night, and it was the first thing she experienced upon awakening each morning. But in spite of the pain, Christine forced herself to get up every morning, exercise, and go to work. She also stayed physically and emotionally connected to her loving husband.

Christine didn't numb or push away the powerful emotions she felt in her chest and stomach. She knew that the deep well of sadness she lived with for many months was grief and not depression. But she did refuse to pursue the "would've/should've/could've" thoughts that kept popping into her head because she knew they would consume her energy. Christine told herself that grief was a part of her life now, a weight that felt like a sack of rocks in her chest.

Christine also made a surprising discovery. Though she still felt grief-stricken most of the time, every now and then she would experience moments of intense pleasure. Simple things like a sunrise, the smell of coffee brewing, the taste of sweet butter on toast, or her husband's touch made her feel wonderful. How was it possible to feel this good—even briefly—she asked herself, when she was so grief-stricken?

As time passed and Christine continued to experience and accept what she felt, her intensely painful feelings faded and were replaced by pleasant feelings that took up more and more space in her life. Eventually, when she became pregnant again, she felt renewed and ready to throw herself back into life.

It may seem ironic, but by experiencing her most painful emotions, Christine was able to get past her pain and move on with her life. When emotions are freely experienced, they fluidly come and go. Throughout the day, you'll see, read, or hear something that momentarily triggers a strong feeling, but if you don't focus on the feeling, it won't last, and a different emotion will soon take its place. When we know how to keep our emotions in balance and don't obsess about what we are feeling, even the most painful and difficult feelings subside and lose their power to control our attention.

When we disconnect from emotions that we find uncomfortable or overwhelming, we automatically shut down the sweet, beautiful emotions that are capable of sustaining us during difficult and challenging times. Emotions that fill us with happiness, laughter, and joy enable us to overcome painful challenges. These uplifting feelings remind us that, even in the worst of times, life can be worthwhile.

THE MORE WE FEEL, THE MORE WE CAN FEEL LOVED

The communication that emotionally connects us to others doesn't necessarily focus on positive feelings. When we are grieving and receive comfort or give comfort to someone who's grieving, the grieving person feels loved. When we empathize with a loved one's fear or anger, or they empathize with our distress, it generates feelings of love.

We can do many things for people we care for, but unless our efforts are accompanied by wordless emotional signals that express our caring interest, our love may have little impact. We don't have to like, or even agree with, the emotions of others to empathize with them. But we can rest assured that the process of emotional communication will create an environment of safety and acceptance that makes people feel loved and brings out the best in them.

Emotions, indeed, are a mixed bag, and that's why we feel very good at times and very bad at other times. Moreover, all of our efforts to limit emotional experiences are misplaced because it isn't emotion that causes us to lose control of ourselves—it's *stress*.

EMOTION IS ONE THING, STRESS IS ANOTHER

We fear and distrust emotion, often believing it's the cause of inappropriate behavior. But the disturbing behavior we fear is caused by our inability to manage stress and the energy we expend trying to avoid our emotions. When we feel threatened and aren't able to relieve our stress, our bodies trigger an instinctual response that permits us to fight, flee, or freeze—but little else. It is this instinctual response, not our emotions, that causes the behaviors we dread.

BEING OUT OF BALANCE IS THE PROBLEM

The anger that's triggered by overwhelming stress is more reflex than emotion. Human emotions are complex, changing and flowing from one instant to the next. A brave man is just as likely to be as frightened as the next person, but he can suddenly experience a rapid succession of other emotions—including care and love—that allows him to be brave. Human emotions also often bring together a mix of feelings. For example, if you're waiting up for a teenager who was supposed to be home hours ago, it's not uncommon to experience a mix of anger, fear, and love. You're angry because your child didn't call, scared that something has happened to her, and relieved and happy when she finally arrives home safely. Human emotions are far more nuanced and complex than instinctual reactions.

We can see this effect in others when they appear to be out of control emotionally. What we can't see, however, is the rapid change that's taking place inside the person that is causing their behavior. When we take a moment to balance our stress and face our emotions, we can think clearly and act appropriately, just like Oliver and Bobby in the following stories.

The man who got hot but kept cool

When **Oliver**'s son called to tell him that he wasn't going to continue college unless his father bought him a car, Oliver felt hurt and angry. He had worked hard for the money he saved to send his son to college and he resented being threatened. Having grown up in a family that was comfortable with a wide range of emotions, Oliver wasn't afraid to get angry. But rather than blow up or get into a confrontation with his son, Oliver remained calm and realized that his son might have more appreciation for money if he worked for it himself. In a composed, pleasant voice, Oliver said, "Go ahead and quit college. That's fine with me." Oliver's response took the wind out of his son's threat and the boy calmed down and apologized.

The woman who wasn't afraid to be fearful

When **Bobby**, who was frail and nearly eighty years old, got the bad news that the elbow she had replaced twenty-five years earlier had completely deteriorated, she was frightened. And when she couldn't find a local surgeon willing to insert a second replacement into someone of her age, her fear increased. But she didn't panic. She had no idea what she should do, but she waited patiently, quieting her fears by spending time with close friends who comforted and supported her. Within a week, one of the doctors who turned her down for surgery called with the name of a reputable surgeon in a nearby town who was willing to do the surgery. She went into surgery relaxed because loving support surrounded her, and she regained the use of her arm.

We can look at Oliver and Bobby and, based on what we see, call them mild-mannered or even-tempered, though this would be inaccurate. How each reacted wasn't due to any innate quality but simply due to their ability to manage anger and stress.

STRESS-FREE EMOTION IS AN EMPOWERING RESOURCE

Today we view emotion very differently than we did fifty years ago. Now we value the emotional regions of the brain for their ability to provide self-awareness, compassion, and perception. Emotion rules our decisions, actions, and personalities. We can lose the thinking parts of our brain without losing our identity, but not the emotional parts.

THERE IS A CONNECTION BETWEEN EMOTIONAL FEELINGS AND PHYSICAL FEELINGS

The searing physical and emotional pain suffered by Christine—the woman who lost her child at birth and coped by experiencing her painful emotions instead of avoiding them—demonstrates that emotion goes hand in glove with physical feelings. Emotions are closely aligned to physical sensations in our bodies; when you experience an emotion, you probably also feel it somewhere in your body, like a tightness in your chest or a churning in your stomach. By paying attention to physical sensations throughout your body, you can recognize your emotions. Moreover, understanding your emotions while enduring pressure can help you make wiser decisions, as the following story shows.

The man who engaged his physical feelings to save his wife's life

Both **Sean** and his wife, Angie, felt torn apart when Angie was diagnosed with a rare brain tumor. Their doctor recommended that they see a colleague who was part of a prestigious neurological team at a leading hospital.

As they prepared to meet the specialist for the first time, Sean could see that Angie was in a daze. They were both frightened, but Sean knew that the fear he felt in his chest and stomach might actually help sharpen his focus, providing he didn't waste energy thinking about some of the scarier possibilities. He was determined to face this meeting with his best decision-making abilities. He listened carefully while he also tuned into the feelings he experienced throughout his body.

The surgeon seemed self-assured and confident as he told them that he had never before seen a tumor quite like Angie's. He didn't think it was malignant, but could not be sure until he performed a biopsy. The one thing the surgeon did seem sure of was that he could remove it. Something about the way the doctor spoke created tension in Sean's throat and shoulders, making him want to move his legs—right out of the office. He didn't know why exactly, but Sean just felt that something was wrong. Then the question hit him: How can this doctor be so sure about what he will do if he isn't sure about what he's going to find?

Sean turned to Angie and said, "I would like you to get at least one other opinion from another surgeon before deciding what to do." That evening Sean spent most of the night researching local brain surgeons who had experience operating on Angie's type of tumor.

The meeting with a second surgeon was an entirely different experience. This doctor asked many more questions and listened very carefully to Sean and Angie's responses. He told them that he had seen and successfully removed tumors like Angie's but needed to run some more tests before making a decision. As it turned out, the mass was benign and, rather than removing it, the doctor chose to leave the tumor alone and follow its progress. The choice turned out to be a good one; Angie was watched for ten years and remained stable.

The intuitive regions of our brain communicate to us through physical sensations, but unless we pay attention to our ever-changing emotional experience, we are apt to miss this important information. When we are under stress, it's easy to lose connection with what we're feeling physically and emotionally in our bodies—especially when we add to our stress by trying to avoid what we feel.

IMPEDIMENTS TO TRUSTING OUR EMOTIONAL EXPERIENCE

We often avoid thinking about or discussing our emotions. Most of us want better self-understanding and better relationships, but the moment someone introduces emotion into a discussion, the conversation abruptly comes to an end; we get defensive, laugh too quickly, or make inappropriate jokes. Yet if no one is watching—in the dark of a movie theater or the bleachers of a sporting event, for example—we are much more comfortable letting emotions such as joy, sadness, or anger flow. Unfortunately, this connection to our emotions is usually fleeting. In the glare of the real world, we suppress those same emotions to the point where we lose touch with them. The sad reality is that most of us distrust emotion.

BOTH HISTORY AND MEMORY CONTRIBUTE TO OUR DISTRUST OF EMOTION

There are both historical and experiential reasons for our discomfort and uncertainty about emotion. For more than 200 years, ecclesiastical, social, and cultural sources regarded emotion as an inferior stepchild to reason. Emotion was thought to reflect our unsophisticated, animal nature, whereas thought was credited with making us reasonable and human. When people behaved badly, their emotions— with help from the devil—were to blame. Reason was given credit for the loftier human virtues, while emotion was blamed for everything we disliked about ourselves.

Science also paid less attention to the emotional parts of the brain until the 1990s. It was then that an extraordinary amount of research disproved most of what had been taught about the brain and the role of emotion. Unfortunately, correcting beliefs that have been held for thousands of years doesn't happen quickly or easily.

In addition to inaccurate beliefs about our emotions, many of us hold on to traumatizing memories that make us fear emotions. Often, these memories occurred early in life when we felt especially vulnerable. We may have been frightened by an earthquake or a parent's outburst; we may have experienced a death in the family or the cruelty of a bully; or we may have felt, for any number of reasons, that life was confusing and unsafe. If someone wasn't there to comfort and calm us, and if we didn't know how to comfort ourselves, we were left feeling that our emotions were hurtful and bad for us. We may have grown up believing that having an emotional experience is too painful, or that there's something wrong or unhealthy about tuning into feelings like sadness, anger, or fear. We may mistakenly think that only pleasant emotions are good for us and, based on these false beliefs, try to build insincere relationships that we believe will make us feel loved, but that ultimately don't.

INFANT EXPERIENCE SHAPES OUR ABILITY TO CONNECT EMOTIONALLY

Our first experiences of feeling loved occur during infancy when we bond emotionally with our primary caretaker. This first falling in love experience shapes our intimate love relationships for the rest of our lives. This concept is also relatively new. Awareness of this emotional process began with a series of remarkable discoveries linking the cohesion of an infant's brain to his or her emotional relationship with a primary caretaker. In *The Neurobiology of Emotional Development*, Dr. Allan N. Schore cites numerous research studies that point to emotional connection as the centerpiece of a person's mental, emotional, social, and physical development.

When an infant's emotional relationship to the primary caretaker creates a feeling of safety and security, this relationship is characterized as secure. Not all relationships, however, are secure. For a variety of reasons that may have to do with health or other circumstances, a primary caretaker may instill instability or fear instead of comfort. When this is the case—and it frequently is—the template for loving relationships becomes insecure. Even good emotions, when unfamiliar, can seem threatening, as Jena and Brad's story illustrates.

The couple whose love followed a pattern that began in infancy

When **Jena** and **Brad** broke up, Jena, who saw herself as intelligent and perceptive, asked herself why she hadn't seen the signs. It was only when she sat down and really thought about her relationship with Brad that she realized there *had* been clues. Toward the end of their relationship, she and Brad had shared less eye contact, he'd touched her less during emotional parts of movies or plays, he'd stopped lingering before saying good night, and he'd stopped talking about their future plans. Jena had continued to do all these things, but Brad had pulled back. Why hadn't she said something, and why hadn't he?

Brad's mother had loved and cared for him when he was a baby, but she was too busy, depressed, and distracted to communicate emotionally with him. Brad, like all infants, tried to send his mother nonverbal emotional messages but eventually gave up when she continued to ignore them. He stopped making an effort to communicate emotionally—a process that involved turning down and turning off his emotions by holding his breath, squeezing parts of his body, and distracting himself. At first, the emotion Brad felt for Jena excited him and felt good. But as these unfamiliar emotions grew stronger, he became increasingly uncomfortable to the point that he felt threatened and needed to end the relationship.

Jena had much the same experience when she was an infant, but she reacted differently. Brad adapted by shutting down his emotions and becoming staunchly independent, whereas Jena always felt emotionally needy. She wore her heart on her sleeve and avoided addressing painful emotional truths that threatened her security. Had Jena been willing to confront Brad when she first felt him pull away, they might have been able to work on the problem. But once he took flight, there was little hope for reconciliation.

Brad may miss Jena when he remembers how happy the two of them were, but unless he makes an effort to reconnect with all his emotions, he's likely to repeat his behavior over and over.

For many of us, this is a familiar story. We fall in love utterly and completely and have every reason to believe that our feelings are shared. Our loved one seems as much in love with us as we are with them. And then without warning, it's suddenly over. They're not as in love with us as we thought they were, and they want to end the relationship. What did we do, or not do, to make this happen?

A GOOD EXPERIENCE CAN BE OVERWHELMING

When we're not used to experiencing an emotion, when it seems strange or unfamiliar, we often want to avoid it—even when it's a pleasant emotion. Emotions that trigger the bonding hormone oxytocin can be intense enough to make us feel out of control. And though the out-of-control feeling may be very pleasurable, it can seem frightening to those unaccustomed to emotional intensity.

People who are used to feeling anxious or hypervigilant can feel threatened when they suddenly feel good. For example, people used to carrying a great deal of weight may report, once they've lost the weight, that they don't feel like themselves or feel very uncomfortable. This doesn't mean that we can't learn to get comfortable with emotions that are unfamiliar—including feelings we like as well as dislike.

It would take effort on Brad's part to reconnect to his emotions, but he could do it. Even if we didn't experience successful emotional communication in infancy, we can still learn these skills. But first, we need to learn how to recognize and manage the stress response that's behind most of the behavior we equate with uncontrolled emotion.

UNREGULATED STRESS MAY DISABLE EMOTIONAL RESPONSIVENESS

Unregulated stress triggers instinctual biological responses that shut down emotional awareness, restricting our emotional responses and making us act in ways that we regret. The stress response draws on anger and fear for motivation, and because of this, our behavior appears to be driven by emotion. In fact, what's happening is a reflection, not of emotion run amok but of someone who has become overwhelmed by stress. To better understand the differences between complex human emotion that flows and instinctual stress responses, let's examine the nature of stress.

Sometimes, stress is a good thing; it keeps us energized and interested in what we're doing. It's only when our stress levels are out of balance that stress becomes problematic. Low, unregulated stress can create feelings of listlessness and depression. High, unregulated stress can trigger responses that have us grinding our teeth, spacing out, or becoming rigid. When we feel safe, we are experiencing the amount of stress we need to stay calm and alert. But when we feel threatened, our nervous systems rapidly make sweeping changes in our bodies that enable us to protect ourselves by fighting, fleeing, or freezing. When we feel helpless and hopeless—as well as frightened—the stress response may get stuck and we can become traumatized for weeks, months, or many years.

TRAUMATIC STRESS IS EMOTION THAT IS FROZEN IN HOPELESSNESS AND HELPLESSNESS

For tens of thousands of years—as humans evolved—our nervous systems, in concert with loving relationships that enabled us to override stress, helped us meet our needs for survival. In a modern world, filled with threats that are now more mental than physical, this self-regulating system faces new challenges.

To begin with, many of us may not realize how stressed we really are. In addition to the role that chronic stress can play in our lives, there is good reason to believe that trauma is much more common than most of us realize, especially early-life trauma. When we're young and helpless, we can be traumatized by events that have nothing to do with abuse or neglect. These may include falls or sports injuries, surgery (especially in the first three years of life), the sudden death of someone close, a car accident, the breakup of a significant relationship, a humiliating or deeply disappointing experience, or the discovery of a life-threatening illness. Traumatic stress disconnects us from the flow of our emotions and in turn disables our ability to feel loved.

EMOTION FULFILLS ITS PROTECTIVE PURPOSE WHEN STRESS IS IN BALANCE

When you learn to balance and regulate stress, you can prevent emotions from overwhelming you. By staying connected to your physical feelings, you can learn to recognize stress that has become too extreme and bring it back into balance. Once you're able to do this, you can comfortably open yourself up to emotions that may have seemed threatening in your past, and connect with them on an ongoing basis.

What you need are the tools that allow you to quickly relieve stress, remain emotionally available, and stay focused. Part Three of *Feeling Loved* provides you with such tools. But first, it's important to understand the obstacles you can face in being able to use these tools.

Part II

BARRIERS THAT STAND
IN THE WAY OF GETTING
THE KIND OF LOVE WE NEED

Part Two of Feeling Loved *examines common practices that create a barrier to giving or receiving the feelings of love we need.*

We are captivated today by simplified solutions to complicated problems that have puzzled us forever: What can we do to feel good, to have friends, and to entertain ourselves? Of course, we need and want these things, and there is nothing inherently wrong about taking a less complicated way to obtain them. But when problems are not uniform or simple, the solutions themselves, such as taking SSRI antidepressants for mild or moderate depression, or relying on the Internet and social media for friendship and love, can become problematic.

Many of the habits of mind and interests we have developed in a complex, technologically engaging world stretch us beyond our limits. By not meeting our need for face-to-face human contact that conveys caring and makes us feel safe, we are stressing ourselves. As we increasingly look for quick solutions, and our lifestyles become faster paced and more reliant on technology, we end up feeling less happy and less fulfilled. When your need is to feel safe, override stress, and experience happiness and fulfillment, the slower and less simple solution may equal more.

CHAPTER 3

Medication Can Be
an Uneasy Solution
to Complex Problems

IN THE 1950S, HEALTH PROFESSIONALS BEGAN focusing on the use of medications to overcome depression and other common mental health problems. Then in 1987, with great fanfare, Prozac was introduced. Prozac—a selective serotonin reuptake inhibitor, or SSRI—was the first of its kind: an antidepressant that promised to be more cost-effective than long-term therapy and could be dispensed easily. It also claimed to offer fast and permanent relief for depression. Twenty years later, millions of people all over the world, including one in every ten Americans, take Prozac or other SSRIs.

Today, we know that antidepressant medication alone is rarely enough to overcome common mental health problems. We also know that while these drugs benefit severely depressed people, they have a nonexistent to negligible impact on milder forms of depression. Moreover, because these medications are intended to blunt the emotional pathways in the brain, those taking them feel less. By blunting our emotions, it becomes more difficult to experience uplifting feelings like joy. It is harder to recognize and reconnect with the inspiring, energizing physical and emotional feelings we need to experience in order to feel loved.

NO ONE SHOULD HAVE TO LIVE WITH DEPRESSION

Depression isn't a one-size-fits-all feeling. It takes many forms, but all of them share some commonality—the experience of being separate, frozen, exhausted, uninspired, and adrift in a world that appears to lack meaning and purpose. In the dark world of depression, thoughts become weapons that we use against ourselves with constant reminders that we are undeserving and unlovable. Even in its far more common milder and moderate forms, depression is an affliction that hurts, both emotionally and physically. For some depressed men and women, rage is the only way to protest at what is happening, and sometimes that rage turns deadly and the person may become suicidal or homicidal. But in our understandable desire to free ourselves from depression's crippling influence, we continue to make choices that, instead of making things better, frequently make things worse.

TOO GOOD TO BE TRUE

When we were first introduced to SSRIs, they seemed like a miracle. We were told that this new group of medications could correct the "bad" brain chemistry that caused depression by focusing on serotonin, a compound in the brain that ferries signals between nerve cells. And they worked; SSRIs seemed to provide relief from depression with less risk of overdose and fewer debilitating side effects. Even if it took a few weeks for the pills to kick in, a short wait was nothing compared to months or years of living under a cloud of depression. From the beginning, however, there were problems. Most notably, there is no way to identify a low or normal level of serotonin in the brain. Yes, it's true that antidepressant drugs such as Prozac increase serotonin levels in the brain, but this doesn't mean that depression is caused by a serotonin shortage. Aspirin may cure a headache, but that doesn't mean that the headaches are caused by aspirin deficiency.

After years of new research, it now appears that there are many other biological, social, and psychological contributors to depression. These include inflammation, elevated stress hormones, immune system suppression, nutritional deficiencies, abnormal activity in certain parts of the brain, and shrinking brain cells. In addition, there are other major factors like isolation, lack of exercise, and poor diet that contribute to depression. These are things that we can actually change without the aid of medication. There is proof that, for the vast majority of people with mild to moderate forms of depression, lifestyle choices, like exercise, and other non-drug therapeutic interventions, can lift depression as effectively as medication.

TRADING WHAT SOUNDS GOOD FOR WHAT FEELS GOOD

Antidepressants reduce bad feelings. That sounds great, but antidepressants also reduce good feelings, which is a problem. All antidepressant medications blunt both the pain and pleasure centers in the brain, including all of the reward pathways. This means that though we will feel less intensely sad or angry, we will also feel less joy, happiness, motivation, meaning, purpose, and connection to others and ourselves. This makes it harder to feel loved and make others feel loved. We are fortunate to have emotion-altering medications when we need them to save lives, but continued use of medications that blunt emotions and limit our connections to others can also have disastrous effects on our lives, as Walter's story exemplifies.

The man who needed to be restrained—but not forever

Walter was one of my very first clients, someone I first met in the short-term group I led as a student-in-training.

After I graduated and left the agency that trained me, Walter found me and asked if I could treat him privately. He was a gentle, soft-spoken teddy bear of a man who seemed painfully shy. His desire to begin a journey of self-exploration pleased me, but by the end of our first session, I knew that Walter's problems were more serious than I had imagined.

Walter led an exceptionally solitary life, living alone in a terribly cluttered, dark apartment. He had no pets or friends, and he didn't know how to make conversation or reach out to others. The only people he saw, aside from his coworkers, were sex workers. In our second session, Walter told me that his coworkers disliked him and how much this hurt and enraged him.

By our third meeting, I knew I had to ask some hard questions: Was he angry enough to want to hurt his coworkers, and if he was, did he have a real plan that he could execute? As I listened I did my best to control my fear and stay focused as Walter calmly told me that he had purchased guns and ammunition and was planning to use them. Fortunately, there was a mental health center that I could call for help in situations like this. A social worker, nurse, and psychiatrist immediately went to Walter's home and talked him into placing himself in a local hospital and taking medications to help protect him and others.

Walter's situation posed the kind of threat that brain-altering medications were designed to immediately address. The medications—when first introduced—were described as "emotional straitjackets" and represented a huge breakthrough in the mental health field. With this type of pharmacological help, someone who posed a threat to themselves or others could more readily be treated at a local hospital. Walter's condition improved almost immediately. I called as soon as I was permitted, though I had been told Walter wouldn't want anything to do with me because I had reported him. That was not the case, however, and he asked me to visit because he had something to show me. In spite of what had happened, I liked Walter and felt there was good in him, so I agreed to come.

When I saw Walter, he told me that when his coworkers heard he was in the hospital they pitched in and bought him a gift. Proudly showing me the lovely card and shirt, he said sheepishly, "I guess they do like me and I was wrong to think I didn't matter to them." I could see how strongly the gift had impacted him because he was so much more self-revealing. He talked to me for the first time about his lonely childhood and the family that hadn't contacted him in years. When I left Walter that day, I was hopeful. In a short period of time he had made great strides in realizing that the world was not as hostile and unfriendly as he had imagined. Though I would no longer be seeing him, I assumed that Walter would continue down a positive path with the psychiatrist who had been assigned to him in the hospital.

I expected that to be the last I saw of Walter, but three years later I recognized him in a synagogue. What I saw made me very sad. Walter sat alone in the back corner of the room, slumped expressionless in his chair. He had gained at least fifty pounds and looked every bit like someone still in a straitjacket. This wasn't my understanding of how the emotion-altering medications were going to be used. Of course, people need constraints if they pose a danger to themselves or others. But given the brain's ability to make positive changes, why didn't Walter's treatment include more than just medication?

HOW MUCH CONSTRAINT DO WE NEED?

Millions upon millions of people all over the world take antidepressants, and many of them remain on these medications, in one form or another, indefinitely. The same family of medications is also used to lower anxiety, and all of these medications come with the possibility of persistent and disabling side effects. Moreover, the vast majority of people who take antidepressants do so for moderate to low levels of depression that non-drug interventions, without side effects, are as likely to relieve. Additionally, most of these medications are prescribed not by mental health professionals who are trained to look for the underlying causes of depression, but by general practitioners who traditionally receive little mental health training. Unfortunately, general practitioners often lack the time and expertise needed to explore the underlying causes of a patient's depression, or the time necessary to observe how the medication changes the patient's social and emotional behavior.

There is no question that medication has an important role to play in preserving health in certain situations. But what happens when we continue to take something we no longer need? If this is the case, we may be forever living with a cast that once helped us mend a broken bone but serves no purpose now that the bone is healed—other than to constrain our movement. One of the most serious and persistent side effects of taking antidepressants often goes unnoticed. Medications that blunt emotions interfere with our connection to the people we are closest to and are most important to us. They make it harder to create and sustain relationships that make us feel loved because these medications make it more difficult to relate emotionally to others.

HOW MEDICATION AFFECTS OUR RELATIONSHIPS

Loneliness and isolation make our brains less coherent. Social ties that contribute to our ability to love and feel loved strengthen us and ground us in reality, helping us stay both physically and emotionally healthy. We now know that the human brain is not only a lot more emotional than we formerly believed, but is far more social as well. Our brains are structured to connect to others, and to be affected by, influenced by, and concerned about others.

OUR SOCIAL AND EMOTIONAL LIVES ARE TWO SIDES OF THE SAME COIN

Human survival depends on our ties to friends and family. World Health Organization studies of people around the world reveal that there is a direct correlation between close-knit families and communities, and all aspects of health. Some of the poorest men and women on Earth who have strong social ties enjoy greater health and happiness than those who have far greater material and intellectual advantages. Communities with very strong social ties are often happier, much like the Okinawan community in Japan, where many people live healthily and happily beyond the age of a hundred. Both old and young people often find emotional fulfillment in a lifestyle based on connecting to nature, loving others, and feeling loved by one another. Emotion is the glue that makes meaningful and fulfilling connections possible. When we make choices that dim emotional awareness, we make it harder to recognize, understand, and relate to others. Loving and feeling loved is a social and emotional process. When we blunt the emotional parts of our brains, as Stephen does in the following story, we diminish our ability to preserve emotionally fulfilling relationships.

The man who lost and regained his spark

When **Stephen**'s boss asked him to move across the country to Chicago, he left behind his family and friends and everything he knew and loved. Stephen was heartbroken to be separated from his family, but he and his wife, Sally, decided to have their kids complete the school term before moving. As the months dragged by, Stephen missed his wife and children more and more.

Never one who enjoyed being alone, he found it harder to return each night to his quiet, lonely apartment, and he began seeking company at a local bar.

He started by drinking just one or two beers, but soon he was drinking unhealthy amounts of alcohol every night. When Sally realized what Stephen was doing, she became concerned. She immediately suspected her husband was depressed and suggested he see a doctor. The trip to a local general practitioner ended with Stephen being prescribed antidepressants. Within a few weeks, the medications began taking the edge off his loneliness and lifted his depression. He could now stay home at night and watch television and not feel so isolated. This was cheaper and more responsible than going to a bar, but the medication also made him less motivated. He stopped exercising, and when he wasn't working, he spent most of his time in front of the TV feeding a larger and larger appetite.

Months passed and Stephen's life remained static while he waited for Sally and the kids to arrive. Eventually the school term ended and the family reunited. They moved into a larger and more comfortable apartment expecting their life together to be as good as it had in the past, but it wasn't. Sally loved Stephen, but he had changed so much that she felt she hardly knew him. It wasn't just the weight gain that made him look different; she missed the spark that she used to feel, even the occasional spark of irritation that helped make their relationship exciting. They had always been so close, nodding and sharing a smile when one of the children acted especially adorably, or making eye contact to acknowledge a secret or memory between the two of them. Now Stephen was more even-tempered, but he was also less reachable. He didn't enjoy doing things the way he used to, and he was less passionate.

Sally told Stephen how she felt, suggesting the medications might be contributing to the distance between them. Stephen agreed to talk to his doctor about coming off the antidepressants. He reasoned that depression shouldn't be an issue now, so why should he need to take antidepressant medication? Withdrawing from the medication turned out to be much longer and harder than expected. Though Stephen followed his doctor's advice and slowly cut back on the dosage, he felt anxious, as well as depressed, for weeks. He was also plagued with flu-like symptoms that made it difficult to work. During this rough time, he was often argumentative and hard to live with. However, the gradual return of positive feelings between Stephen and Sally kept him from reversing his decision to quit antidepressants. As Stephen tapered off the medication and started exercising again, both he and Sally experienced the return of their deep connection that once more made them feel loved.

When emotions are blunted, our social and emotional connections to others are dimmed. But there are viable alternatives to antidepressants. Had Stephen known that lifestyle changes and therapy could have been as effective for treating his depression as medication, he might have opted for them and saved himself a painful process of withdrawal. Of course, there are times when a partner is ill or disabled and out of necessity needs more support than usual. But if a typical relationship is going to flourish—if both partners are going to feel loved—they will need a full palette of emotions with which to communicate and share experiences.

ANTIDEPRESSANTS MAY BE HARD TO DISCONTINUE

Stopping an antidepressant medication can be difficult. Changes can occur throughout the body that result in severe emotional and physical problems. Problems can include loss of appetite, nausea, vomiting, diarrhea, and flu-like symptoms such as a runny nose, sweating, muscle aches, and fever. Symptoms like restlessness, insomnia, dizziness, lightheadedness, and anxiety can also occur. Emotional states like depression and anxiety are sometimes confused with a relapse or reoccurrence of the original illness. It takes time for our bodies to adjust to the *absence* of any drug—some more so than others. Antidepressants can help people over rough spots. There are times when we can't recover without slowing down and resting. Sometimes it's appropriate to take a time-out, rest, and recuperate, but there are also times when we need to wake up, get motivated, and take action.

A WORD OF CAUTION

When taking any medication, there is always the risk that it may not have the expected results or that the medication may actually do more damage than good. This is especially true with the dangerous risk factors associated with antidepressant medications. In some people, antidepressant use causes an increase, rather than a decrease, in feelings of depression—and with it, an increased risk of suicide. Children and young adults are at the greatest risk for this devastating side effect.

DRAWING ON THE BEST OF MANY POSSIBILITIES

Finding a balance in life is often the key to maintaining health. For example, millions of children in the U.S. currently take medications that have not thoroughly been tested on children. A more balanced approach might be to use these medications as a window of opportunity for making lifestyle and other non-drug interventions, as demonstrated by the preteen in the following story.

The girl who found her way home

Deborah came from a picture-perfect family that talked a lot about family values. Her mother quit a job she loved to be a full-time mom when Deborah was born. Both parents doted on Deborah, indulging her every whim. But though her parents continued to focus on her, their kind attention to one another stopped. Deborah fell asleep to the sounds of heated arguments. Hearing the things her parents said to one another hurt and had a chilling effect on Deborah, but she grew used to it. During puberty, however, when everything about her was changing and she felt so vulnerable, Deborah made a crushing discovery.

One morning, Deborah's school bus passed an outdoor café where she saw her father at one of the tables flirting with another woman. From then on, she looked for her father at the café every day, and repeatedly saw him with different women. If he didn't love her mother, Deborah reasoned, maybe he didn't love her either. A bad situation got worse when Deborah worked up the courage to tell her father what she had seen. Her dad responded to her accusations with anger and self-righteousness, telling her that she had imagined what she saw. He said she was an awful, horrid person to say such things.

Deborah felt that her life was falling apart and she was going crazy. Her stomach hurt so badly she could barely eat, and she started having panic attacks. Nothing was the same at school or with her friends. Nothing seemed to matter, and she began spiraling down a dark hole. Things came to a head when her parents found her sitting in the freezing cold at the edge of the home's second-story roof, wearing just a thin nightgown. When Deborah refused to leave the roof, her parents called the police, and Deborah was taken to the psychiatric ward at a local hospital. Since the doctors thought she might be suicidal, they watched her very carefully and gave her medications to prevent her from hurting herself.

Deborah's antidepressants took the edge off her hopelessness and helplessness, and she began seeing a therapist. Her therapist had been a troubled kid herself and was a very good fit for Deborah. She gave her a great deal of face-to-face support and helped Deborah put what had happened into perspective. She also helped Deborah build emotional skills to navigate painful and frightening situations and to restore her self-confidence.

Deborah's parents, heartbroken by what had happened, felt responsible and went into therapy. Her dad apologized to both Deborah and her mother for his words and behavior. Both parents realized they loved one another and neither wanted to break up their family. As each of them became aware of how unsafe and unloved the other felt, their relationship began to resume its former closeness. While Deborah strengthened her relationship with herself, her parents strengthened theirs with one another.

As Deborah built self-confidence and her family's relationships stabilized, her depression and anxiety diminished. She learned the value of exercise and meditation in managing stress and overwhelming emotions. Eventually, Deborah asked to be taken off the medications, explaining that they made her feel flat. She could see that those around her were very happy, and she, too, wanted to feel this pleasure. Slowly, under the watchful eye of a psychiatrist, Deborah cut back on her dosages, eventually discontinuing all medication. The process wasn't especially difficult for the active teenager. Because Deborah used the time taking antidepressants as a window of opportunity for new learning, she began to feel loved again.

THE IMPORTANCE OF A BALANCED APPROACH

Lifestyle changes like exercise and meditation can have a better chance of reducing depression and anxiety than antidepressants, especially in the long term. For the vast majority of people who remain functional with mild to moderate depression, lifestyle changes can provide tremendous benefits. Everything we've learned about the roles exercise, diet, sufficient sleep, and fulfilling relationships play in maintaining physical health is even truer when it comes to sustaining mental health. It can be harder to develop new healthier lifestyles while taking medications that blunt motivation, but with support and encouragement, it can be done. It's hard to feel loved or make others feel loved when we feel helpless and down, but a simple solution—like taking antidepressants—can make it even harder. A balanced perspective values experiencing intensely positive feelings as much as it values blunting feelings of hopelessness. A balanced approach also takes into consideration the role stress plays in blocking our social and emotional needs. It sees the overarching effect that fulfilling—or failing to fulfill—these needs has on our health and well-being. This approach also underlines the importance of being fully connected to the emotions that can relieve stress and inform and guide our relationships, plus increase our ability to feel deeply loved.

CHAPTER 4

Virtual Connections Can Cause Greater Disconnection

A TYPICAL OBSERVATION IN OUR MODERN, TECHNOLOGY-OBSESSED WORLD

It's Sunday morning. I'm seated across from my husband in a sunny neighborhood restaurant taking pleasure in his attention. I'm aware of the softness in his face and the way he leans toward me when he speaks. When he leaves to go to the restroom, I notice a man sitting alone at a nearby table. Head down, he speaks quietly into his cell phone. When the friendly waiter comes by to take his order, he stops talking and speaks to the waiter, but doesn't look up.

There is an empty table to my right and a family of four—a mother, father, and two little boys—heads in our direction. They seat themselves just as our food arrives. In the time it takes our waiter to set the plates on our table, both the mother and youngest son have their phones in their hands and are texting and playing games. The father sits and stares at nothing in particular. The other boy—an especially beautiful child—catches my gaze and I smile at him, but he doesn't smile back. Instead, he appears both sad and embarrassed.

VIRTUAL CONNECTIONS
DON'T CREATE FULFILLING LIVES

Motivated by the increased speeds of the Internet and rapid evolution of social networks, many of us go online every day to "connect" with people, information, and entertainment. We are spending not just minutes here and there, but rather hours each and every day in front of screens, both big and small.

Technology is amazing and our lives are certainly more comfortable because of it. Portable devices like tablets, smartphones, and laptops have made it possible to have steady virtual relationships with family, loved ones, colleagues, and new acquaintances in distant parts of town, distant cities, and distant countries. At the same time, it's not uncommon to see two people sitting at the same table, silently tagging each other in photos on their phones instead of having a real conversation and enjoying each other's company. And when you see a situation like this, it's hard not to wonder if all these virtual connections are being overused.

By being so deeply but virtually connected for so many hours of the day, are we forgetting how to connect to each other in person? Do our tablets and phones make our lives better, or do they exhaust us and add to our stress? Is social media replacing the emotionally driven, nonverbal communication we need to connect in a meaningful way to others? Are virtual connections affecting our ability to communicate with others in ways that permit us to feel loved and make others feel loved? To better understand these questions, let's compare online relationships and real, in-person relationships.

SCREENS DON'T ALLOW US TO COMMUNICATE NONVERBALLY

Before we knew any words to speak, we used emotional and nonverbal cues to communicate. We smiled, frowned, and waved our arms. We stamped our feet, raised our shoulders, and pointed our fingers. We were able to understand each other without words because we could still connect with eye contact, movements, and other nonverbal cues.

How would a baby react to being shown a highly expressive and emotional email message with emoticons and bolded, capital letters, and a dozen exclamation points? Would the baby understand the excitement, or would he or she simply try to play with the keyboard or suck on the mouse? An email—even when positive and expressive—means nothing to an infant. But if we sit in front of a baby and use nonverbal means of communication, like facial expressions or sounds, that baby will respond immediately. Adults still rely heavily on this inborn responsiveness to physical communication. This sensitivity to faces, bodies, voices, and touch remains as important to us now as it did when we were infants.

Nonverbal communication constantly takes place when we are with others, but it is easy to miss or forget. People who don't pay attention to the subtleties of wordless communication may miss it entirely. Nevertheless, the field of developmental psychology credits human relatedness to nonverbal communication. In virtual conversations, however, most of the complex wordless information that permits us to know and understand each other is lost.

VIRTUAL CONNECTIONS CAN'T DUPLICATE THE COMPLEXITY OF IN-PERSON COMMUNICATION

While the exact percentages may be debated, at least 75 percent of all communication is nonverbal. Our brains are wired to receive wordless signals from others that tell us if a person is friendly or interested in us. This signaling registers in the brain at such remarkable speeds that while we're sending in-person messages, we are also receiving important messages. The expressions we read when we look into another person's eyes—or what we see when we watch what's happening with their lips, how they tilt their head or hold their hands—tell us more about what the person thinks and feels than any of the words they exchange. Also, the rise or fall in the tone and intensity of someone's voice and how they do, or do not, reach out and touch us delivers additional information rarely conveyed by words alone. When we have a conversation with another person over lunch, for example, and receive a nonverbal signal that indicates our communication isn't having the desired effect, we can instantly make a correction and help build a stronger, more successful relationship.

When we communicate virtually, however, there is a significant disconnect between the sending and receiving process. It's difficult to interpret tone, sarcasm, or genuine excitement or disapproval in an email or text. Though the actual time lapse between virtual sending and receiving can be very brief, our brains find the mismatch stressful.

The capacity of the brain to pick up billions of bits of sensory information and connect them to billions of other bits makes in-person communication unique. This isn't something we can do online, even when using Skype or video conferencing applications. What follows are two stories about grandparents who want very much to bond emotionally with their grandkids. Their goals are the same, but because the means of communication is virtual in one example and face-to-face in the other, the outcomes are very different.

Grandparents who wanted to connect online but couldn't

Ed and **Judy** were doting grandparents who felt very close to their children and grandchildren. When their son, Scott, and his family moved out of the country so that Scott could advance his career, they were heartbroken. Scott and his wife, Kerri, had three little children: Ellie, who was four years old; her younger brother, Steve, who was two and a half; and six-month-old Simon. Desperate to connect and keep in touch with their grandchildren, Ed and Judy set up a weekly meeting on Skype.

Devoting every Saturday evening to a virtual relationship with their grandchildren required some sacrifice on their part, but Ed and Judy didn't complain. As far as they were concerned, time with their grandchildren was the most important part of the week. They watched the little ones at play and tried to make conversation, but it wasn't easy. Ellie would remember bits of information from their previous online conversation, but Steve, the two-and-a-half-year-old, didn't have the attention span to look into the camera and answer Ed and Judy's questions.

Each week, Ed and Judy's affection for the children grew as they noted changes in the children's development and behavior. Their grandchildren, however, didn't experience these meetings in the same way. The two-dimensional images they saw on the screen were unreal and a bit strange. In fact, the Skype sessions reminded the kids of the games they played on their iPads and computers. Because these meetings were virtual, Saturday evenings meant much more to the grandparents than they did to the kids.

Ed and Judy's experience is common in a world where families are routinely separated by thousands of miles. The relationship-building experience they had with their grandchildren was much different than the one I witnessed recently between a grandfather and his grandchild while I was out taking a morning walk.

A priceless interaction between a grandfather and granddaughter

Viewed from afar, the scene down the block seemed odd. A white-haired man sat in the middle of the sidewalk with his legs around a stroller that faced him. As I approached, I saw that a small child sat in the stroller and that she and the older gentleman were at eye level. The two of them were so engrossed in one another that neither noticed me as I stopped to watch.

Face to face and eye to eye, the baby put her finger on the older man's nose. He followed by placing one of his fingers on the tip of her nose and was rewarded with a smile. Next, she began exploring his mouth with her fingers and giggled delightedly when he put one of his large fingers on her lips. With an open-mouthed expression of delight, the grandfather broke into laughter. The baby became even more excited and started clapping, first her hands, then his cheeks.

I continued to watch, and every now and then the baby stopped playing, looked away, and took a needed break. (An infant's nervous system needs to rest more frequently than an adult's.) When this happened, the grandfather followed her lead and stopped playing. This was a dance the baby led, and she seemed to know it. After a pause, she started up again, exploring her sense of touch, taste, and hearing with great enthusiasm. I don't know how long the two of them sat in the middle of the sidewalk sharing this joy; neither of them noticed as I left smiling to myself, grateful to have witnessed this charming example of how we make one another feel loved.

In-person, physical interactions lead to fulfilling emotional connections. Communication pales on a flat screen, as the subtleties in timing and pace that in-person communication allows are difficult to replicate online. True eye-to-eye contact isn't possible when you're looking at a screen. Nor are there opportunities for exploring sensations like taste, touch, and smell, which simply can't be duplicated virtually.

SENSORY AND EMOTIONAL EXPERIENCE IS LIMITED ONLINE

There is an important difference between looking at someone and looking carefully enough to pick up the subtle, nonverbal cues that reveal what the person feels. When we look into one another's eyes and pick up the subtle changes taking place in the face and body near us, we gather information that cannot be gathered from a virtual distance. There are dozens of muscles in the face that a flat computer screen obscures. Skype or services like GoToMeeting don't catch the subtle changes taking place in someone's forehead or in the tiny muscles that surround the eyes, nose, and mouth. In person, our brains register these subtleties. Also, as we touch, smell, and taste one another with a kiss or hug, we share sensory and emotional experiences that virtual realities are not likely to ever offer. The close relationship between emotion and sensory experience is reflected by the idea that the emotional part of the brain probably evolved from the sense of smell.

Relaxed, mutually shared nonverbal communication that makes us feel safe and encourages exploration also makes us feel loved. Developmental psychologists have referred to the joyous, sensory-rich experience that infants share with their caretakers as "the falling in love experience." This early experience of falling in love creates a template of expectation for future love relationships. With this in mind, I wonder what effect virtual communication is having on our children?

As I watch parents and caretakers spend more time watching, reading, and listening to their electronic devices instead of reading to, watching, and listening to their children, I think about the epidemic rise in childhood problems like ADD/ADHD, learning disabilities, and autism spectrum disorders. Is there a relationship between the two? Are there serious repercussions for young children when caretakers focus significant amounts of time on their phones or tablets? Are there ramifications for our relationships and our health when we devote large amounts of time to virtual interests instead of in-person communication?

PLUGGED IN AND TUNED OUT

Virtual communication has been accused of creating more narcissistic and less empathic individuals. I don't think this is necessarily true, but virtual communication definitely is less emotionally fulfilling than in-person communication. It's a quicker, easier process, and dozens of emails and text messages can be sent and received in a matter of minutes. Because virtual communication doesn't rely on sensory information and nonverbal cues, however, it invites plenty of misunderstandings. It's hard to know exactly what the other person is thinking or feeling. This is especially true when messages are not strictly informational and contain emotional overtones. Does a message contain too much or not enough information? Does it have a positive or negative effect? Does the recipient feel overwhelmed or underwhelmed? Of course, questions like these can be asked and answered in an email, but this rarely happens.

Nonverbal in-person communication is the only way we can relate to infants or those unable to understand our words. Though less obvious, wordless communication is equally important when we are connecting to adults. All relationships—from the most important to the least important—draw on emotionally driven, sensory-rich, wordless communication. The success or failure of our ability to move and influence others depends more on what we say without words than what we say with them. This is as true in the workplace as it is anywhere else in our lives.

How we earn a living has become an increasingly virtual experience. Many of us not only work on computers in the office, but we also socialize with our colleagues online, even when they sit just a few cubicles away. When people used to meet in person at the water cooler or the lunch room during work breaks, they'd take the time to interact face-to-face. Today, however, people are more likely to keep their attention firmly fixed on a smartphone or tablet instead of interacting with each other. Moreover, as we spend more time shaping our brains online, we lose touch with how important our in-person connections are, as the following story demonstrates.

Substituting online communication for in-person connections

Dan was thrilled when he landed a job as an engineer. Taking the job meant he would have to move several hundred miles from his hometown, but he was young and up for the adventure. His plan was to keep in touch with friends and family by email or on Facebook and Twitter.

At first, Dan's expertise and attention to detail was appreciated at work. This began to change, however, when Dan's boss urged him to quicken his pace with certain projects. More and more pressure was put on Dan to work faster, even when this meant doing unprofessional, sloppy work. He worked as fast as he could, but soon his boss began sending a steady stream of emails complaining to others that Dan was working too slowly. Adding to Dan's frustration was the supervisor's unwillingness to talk in person about the problem, communicating with him only through email. Far from motivating him, the pressure only made it increasingly difficult for him to focus, and Dan fell further and further behind. In a vain effort to meet his boss's demands, Dan began taking work home at night. As his tension built, Dan tried to forget his troubles by going online. Soon, Dan was plugged in night and day.

The more time Dan spent plugged in, the more wired, stressed, and fatigued he became. He fell further and further behind at work. The company didn't fire him, but his salary and benefits were reduced.

Dan was too embarrassed and ashamed to talk to anyone about what was going on. When friends or loved ones contacted him, he told them everything was great. The fact that there was little opportunity to meet face-to-face with anyone at work added to his isolation. Without the support of people who cared about him, Dan's life began to stray off track. He retreated into a world of computer games, television, and online shopping. Weekends were spent in front of the computer or texting people he was never likely to meet in person. No one who cared about Dan was near enough to notice the dark circles under his eyes from a lack of sleep. No one was there to see that he had retreated into a virtual world that prevented him from feeling loved.

Dan's family began to suspect that something was wrong when he didn't have enough money to fly home for the holidays. Given Dan's salary—the salary they thought he was still making—it didn't make sense that he couldn't afford the price of a ticket. Dan's parents made it a point to visit him as soon as they could. When they did, Dan's problems immediately became obvious and his family intervened. With support that made him feel loved, Dan recognized he was in a dead-end situation at work. He quit his job and began looking for work that would be a better fit for his work ethic and social needs. It took a while to find the right position, and Dan worked odd jobs until he found what he needed, when he was eventually hired at a small engineering firm.

The new job didn't pay as well as the old one, but Dan felt so much better about himself that it didn't matter. He felt appreciated and respected by his new boss, who made it a point to look him in the eye whenever he had something important to discuss. He worked face-to-face with coworkers who met in person to discuss work-related challenges. To his surprise, his colleagues also met after work to play and relax together. Dan joined the company's cycling club and made new friends playing cards. In an environment with people who showed in-person interest and respect, Dan did his best work.

Our needs for social and emotional connection don't turn *off* when we're at work. To be our best, most-productive selves, we need to be both focused and relaxed. The feeling of safety that inspires the best in us is the product of supportive, in-person, nonverbal communication. We need to experience the look, feel, and sensory awareness that tell us the people we are working with accept and appreciate us. With this reassurance, we tap into our ability to do and be our best. Unfortunately, when this is not the case, it becomes easier and easier to escape into a virtual world.

ONLINE EXPERIENCE CAN BE EXCITING BUT NOT FULFILLING

Many men and women look to the Internet and social networks for emotional fulfillment, but their chances of finding a quick fix for loneliness or boredom aren't very high. Only in-person connection provides the kinds of experiences needed to remain calm and focused and to be socially and emotionally fulfilled.

Being online offers ways to stay in touch and schedule appointments with those we know and care about. In our mind's eye, we can remember being with loved ones and imagine how good that felt. Those with powerful imaginations can hold on to joyous memories and be sustained by them. Most people, however, need more than memories to feel loved. We need in-person experiences that convey the love others feel for us. We need to know what we are feeling even when what we feel is unpleasant. Virtual connections can be pleasurable and even exciting, but there is a difference between excitement and fulfillment. Happiness is an infusion of joy that informs and motivates all parts of our lives; it's not fleeting and it isn't something we get by avoiding feelings we don't like.

WE CAN WORK WITHOUT
JOY BUT WE NEED JOY TO LIVE

Research from the field of positive psychology indicates that it's not necessary to feel good all the time to be happy. We don't have to always like what we're doing as long as there are parts of our lives that we do enjoy and make us happy. Some happy people spend a lifetime in jobs they don't enjoy. But when this is the case, there are other important parts of their lives that make them feel very good—often relationships that make them feel loved.

BEING DOWN IS AN
ESSENTIAL PART OF STAYING UP

More and more people keep busy by staying connected to virtual friends. Social networks can be the start of new in-person friendships, but they can also be a distraction. When you're alone and scrolling through Twitter or Facebook, it's easy to become so consumed by the swiftness and ease of the technology, and so distracted by all the incoming information, that you lose touch with what you're feeling. We become engrossed with what we're looking at and ignore the emptiness in our lives.

When we're preoccupied with our phones, tablets, and computers, it's easy to think that we're doing so much when, in fact, we're accomplishing so little. We need downtime to relax, restore ourselves, and integrate new learning. By staying plugged in, our brains remain on alert and we miss restorative opportunities. Also, after a while everything can seem equally important, making it difficult to make the best choices. By remaining plugged in, we lose touch with emotions that signal a need to slow down or stop and reassess. Virtual technologies, including social media, can prevent us from realizing when it's time to make changes in our lives. When we discover what feels bad, we can begin to feel better.

Fortunately, we don't have to choose between turning on and turning off; we can do both. We can enjoy the fun, excitement, and educational and social opportunities that are available online. We can also learn to turn off this technology when we need to focus on experiences that make us feel loved. We don't have to choose between online or in-person interaction, but we do have to understand what should be expected from each.

YOUR ONLINE FRIENDS AND RELATIONSHIPS MAY NOT ALWAYS BE AS REPORTED

Sensory limitations aren't always a bad thing. Online or virtual experiences with social media, dating sites, text messaging, or chat rooms can fuel our imaginations in clever and creative ways. But spending too much time in these environments, with their sensory limitations, can also lead us astray. Without the opportunity to validate the assumptions we make about other people we interact with online, we can let our imaginations run amok and confuse what we want with what we have. Even if we do eventually meet some people face-to-face after meeting them online, we're often disappointed to find they don't match the descriptions they've given of themselves.

As tempting as it is to let our imaginations color our impressions of others, it's even more tempting to be imaginative when describing ourselves. Online profiles frequently overstate or understate what we see in ourselves. It's easy to stretch the truth or forget about flaws we'd rather not possess in real life. It's important to recognize that if you do this, then your online friends may do this, too. Many hide behind their screen or online personas, and it's anybody's guess as to whether an in-person experience will match the descriptions we put on our online profiles.

Before we can be certain that we've made a new friend or met someone special, we need to know how it feels to be face-to-face with that person. We need to experience in-person attraction and the give and take of in-the-moment friendship. We also need to experience what happens when the two of us strongly disagree. We need to ask:

- Do our new friends or potential lovers go off in a huff?
- Do they stop talking to us?
- Can we work out disagreements?
- Will they apologize when they regret something they've done?

- Will they ask for forgiveness, and can they be forgiving?
- Have we found friends or potential lovers who are able to take as well as give, and give as well as take?

We need to explore all of these questions and more before we can be certain that a friendship or a relationship is a secure one that will make us feel loved.

THE LANGUAGE OF LOVE IS COMMUNICATED IN PERSON

Online, the rich interpersonal qualities afforded by the five senses are lost, as are important opportunities for nonverbal communication. Offline in the real world, your eyes, ears, skin, nose, and tongue can interconnect in wondrous ways. Clusters of sensations make for relationships that are highly robust in emotion and meaning.

We need shared, in-person experiences to assess the value of friendship. We need to hear the change in voice tone when someone who values and cares about us speaks to us. We need to see the affection in their eyes and on their faces. We need to feel our friend's arm on our shoulder or around us when we're cold or sad. We need to see that our friend has started to laugh or cry at the same moment we began laughing or crying. These sensual, nonverbal experiences make us feel valued. And they cannot take place online.

We can meet and chat online, but it's dangerous to make the most important decisions about our relationships in a virtual reality. Normal filters are absent in a fiber optic ether where artificiality and seductiveness reign. We need to discover what being together feels like in a variety of settings. We also need to pick up on cues that tell us how our friend feels being with us when we're not at our best, or when they are not at their best. This *getting to know you* process takes time and the kinds of experiences that aren't available online. The relationships that make us feel loved can begin in front of a screen, but are only sustainable offline.

CHAPTER 5

Too Much Thinking Can
Lead to Not Enough Loving

FROM THE MOMENT WE LEARN TO speak, many of us never stop talking—mostly to ourselves. Day and night, we find ourselves constantly in the recesses of our own minds, lost in our thoughts and imaginations. And as we grow older and life gets busier and more complex, the volume of the chatter inside our heads only gets louder and louder. With all this internal noise and distraction, we miss out on the here and now, and with it, the heartfelt, joyous experiences that take place only when our focus is in the present.

In our rush to do, be, and have so much, we often sideline the less intense and stressful parts of life, disconnecting ourselves completely from our emotions. We become so focused on *what* we're doing that we forget about *how* we're doing. We habitually think more and feel less, separating us not only from each other, but also from ourselves. It's ironic; we believe multitasking and working extra hard brings so much harmony into our lives when, in reality, it can be very stressful. When this happens, we may be figuratively (and occasionally even literally) heading over a cliff.

DEATH BY OVERWORKING

Karoshi—death by overwork—is such a growing problem in Japan that a law was passed in November 2014 aimed at preventing this praenomina from occurring. *Karoshi and the Ethic of Work* is a documentary film that tells the story of a young husband and father who, without warning, loses consciousness and dies while at work. As with other karoshi victims, there is no apparent cause of death. So why would the heart of a healthy twenty-nine-year-old man just stop beating?

Like many in Japan, and all over the world, this husband and father was under tremendous pressure to work overtime and support his family. At one point, the documentary includes home movies of this man and his family taken shortly before he died. As I watched these clips, I believe I saw something that may have contributed to his death, aside from the long work hours. I saw a tall, handsome, well-built man sitting alone, engrossed in his thoughts as his wife and child desperately tried to get his attention. He was so exhausted and inwardly focused that he barely paid attention to his little son, who obviously adored him. He appeared absolutely lost in his mind, disconnected from his emotions, and distracted, which, I believe, contributed to his untimely death.

YOUR UNHEALTHY MENTAL HABITS
CAN CREATE OVERWHELMING STRESS

Thinking inspires and elevates us. The mind is a beautiful thing when we use it to be creative or solve problems. But the mind, or rather how we use it, can be a double-edged sword. It has the amazing ability to open up our worlds so that we can achieve and aspire, but when we choose to think obsessively—to the point of blunting emotional awareness— our thoughts can shut down our worlds and even kill us.

When your life focuses almost exclusively above the bridge of your nose, you are disconnected from the social and emotional parts of your life. Alone in your thoughts, you can easily become self-absorbed and self-centered, losing touch with vital feelings that inform you about yourself and your relationships. Many people get so used to being out of balance that they treat their high levels of stress as nothing out of the ordinary. And this can lead to very serious repercussions.

REMAINING IN OUR HEADS
CAN BLOCK FEELING LOVED

When we're always thinking—always planning, strategizing, multitasking, or worrying—we're locked into a mental process that sets us apart from others. Alone in our thoughts, we miss opportunities to lock gazes with others, failing to see the expression on another's face that could make us feel loved. We miss the falling in love experience of being with someone whose only purpose is to be with us in that moment.

THE DANGER IN TRYING TO DO EVERYTHING AT ONCE

Life, as many of us lead it, amounts to trying to do several things at the same time. We constantly feel compelled to do more, to achieve more, both professionally and personally. And we know that in order to be our best, we have to take care of ourselves and put some time and thought into things like exercise, diet, and appearance. We also have busy social lives with friends, family, spouses, children, and parents.

Given all we do with how little time we have, it's understandable that we want to accomplish several things at once. Why not work out or fix dinner while having a serious conversation with our spouse or one of our kids? Why not shop online or drive the kids to school while talking on the phone to our sister or best friend? We might feel stress and suspect that it has something to do with trying to do too many things at once, but we don't see an alternative, so we keep going.

If we continue to remain lost in our thoughts and plans, we're not going to notice that we're constantly losing ground. We won't notice that life has begun to feel more like a burden rather than a source of joy and well-being. We must stop and ask ourselves: Does doing so much give me more out of life or leave me with less? Is there a relationship between what I'm doing and how tired and disconnected I feel?

Multitasking often causes us to lose the ground we need to feel loved and to make others feel loved. The following story exemplifies why doing more can result in having less.

The woman who did more but got less

Joanna was the picture-perfect modern woman, trying to keep half a dozen balls in the air at all times. Charming, attractive, successful, and popular, she was a hardworking career woman, wife, and mother. She would tell you the only way she accomplished anything was by multitasking; while doing one activity, she thought about or planned another. When her kids were little, she dressed them while thinking about her next work assignment. When she went for a walk with her husband, she thought about what to make for dinner. And when she said "good night" to her family, she planned her schedule for the next morning. Her family sensed her preoccupation even as they appreciated her intelligence and hard work. What they missed, however, was a strong interest in their lives.

Doing several things at the same time seemed natural to Joanna; it was what she had always done. As a child, whenever she felt sad or bad, she retreated into her imagination, making plans for projects and things she wanted to do. Living in her imagination became a habit that served her creativity, but kept her from being in the moment with others or paying close attention to them.

When she was younger, she might have told you she had it all. But as the years went by, she began to wonder if that was true. Did she still have it all? Her relationship with her husband was comfortable and secure, but the tenderness and excitement that originally drew them together no longer existed. He followed her lead, retreating into work and hobbies like golf. Her children showed such promise when they were little, but they grew up to be dependent, insecure adults who didn't seem very connected to anyone or anything. Joanna finally noticed all this disconnection. She missed the feelings she used to share with her husband, and felt guilty about her kids. She asked herself how, if she worked so hard for so much, this had happened.

DOING MORE CAN EQUAL LESS FULFILLMENT

Multitasking, instead of making our lives easier, contributes to our becoming overwhelmed by stress. Scientists say that those who frequently multitask often have more trouble focusing and shutting out irrelevant information, and actually experience more stress. Even after the need for multitasking ends, fractured thinking and lack of focus persist. As we spend our waking hours doing—or thinking about doing—more than one thing at a time, we increase our stress load.

Of course, there is nothing wrong with exploring many of life's possibilities and doing many things. The problem lies in exclusively remaining focused on your thoughts while doing other things, such as connecting with others. You can listen to music as you run, and it may be a good idea to plan an exciting vacation while the dentist is drilling your teeth. But if you're interacting with someone and simultaneously checking your email or planning your weekend, you won't be able to make a real emotional connection. Multitasking and the stress it triggers separate us from the parts of ourselves we need to be emotionally present and self-aware.

THINGS WE DO TO RELAX THAT STRESS US

In a world where a busy and intense life is made to seem better and more exciting, many of the things we do to relax create more stress. Watching hours of TV, staying up all night partying, or going to an action movie, rock concert, or as many events in one night as we can may appeal to our minds as fun and exciting, but may also add to our stress rather than reducing it. An obsession with excitement and fast entertainment leaves many of us exhausted and over-whelmed by what we're doing in an attempt to relax. And it becomes a vicious circle. We try to rest but cannot quiet our thoughts, and this leads us to crave further excitement.

TO BE OR NOT TO BE IN
OUR THOUGHTS AT ALL TIMES

We are born feeling, not thinking. When we're little, we learn words in order to communicate faster with the adult world. This habit continues throughout life; we find we can communicate quickly with our words, but we're not necessarily communicating effectively. As the pace of life accelerates, it's easy to pay less attention to what we're feeling. Awareness of our thoughts overshadows awareness of our feelings. We think more, feel less, and focus increasingly on what has happened or what may happen rather than on what *is* happening. The more we do this, the less aware we are of moment-to-moment experiences. From this heady perspective it's easy to lose control of our fast-paced, crowded, and intense lives.

By responding to experiences from our hearts as well as our heads, we can accomplish more and be more fulfilled, as the following story about Latisha shows.

A woman who does a lot, one thing at a time

Latisha had a demanding job that required long hours of work. She also had a husband, two kids, and a potentially life-threatening illness. In spite of this load, Latisha went from task to task and person to person with energy in her step and a smile on her face. How did she do so much without becoming overwhelmed?

If Latisha had a secret, it was that she did one thing at a time, and she did it with enthusiasm. She loved her job because it gave her the opportunity to make a difference in the lives of children in need. When she was on the clock, those children were all she focused on. When she got home, her attention was fully on her husband and two kids.

Latisha's time management secret seemed ridiculously simple. When she was doing one task, she was not planning another. When she was with one person, she was not thinking about another. Though Latisha was thoughtful and bright, she didn't get absorbed in her thoughts unless a task or person demanded it. She put her heart and head into understanding what was required of her and what she should do. By remaining focused on the people she was with, she let them know how much she cared and was willing to do.

When she was with people who tended to make her life difficult, Latisha relied on the Serenity Prayer. She asked herself, "Is this something I can change or not?" If it wasn't a situation that she had the power to alter, she moved on to the things that she could influence. (The Serenity Prayer: *God grant me the serenity to accept the things I cannot change; courage to change the things I can; and wisdom to know the difference.*) Latisha wasted little time on people or situations she could do nothing about.

Latisha juggled many roles in life by focusing on only one role at a time. She conserved her energy by knowing what was most important. She was also aware of her need to relax in ways that calmed and soothed her. Instead of going to the latest action flick that was full of violence, she went for a run in the park by herself or with her family. By staying focused on what she felt as well as what she was doing, Latisha enjoyed a full and happy life while protecting her health and well-being.

HEADED FOR LONELINESS

Relationships are built on the connections we make in accordance with what happens from one moment to the next. If our intention is to be in a relationship, we can't be somewhere else in our thoughts.

Thinking is a solitary process. We can share our thoughts with others, but we can't focus on others while we're deep in thought because we can't hide our preoccupation with something internal. The expressions on our faces, the tone of our voices, and the way we move tells people if we are truly with them or if we're absorbed in our own thoughts and mainly with ourselves. If you are preoccupied with yourself and spending time with an acquaintance you don't know very well, chances are that the person won't tell you what they see, but they will surely feel it. Even if you're with your spouse or best friend, if they see you lost in your head or constantly checking your phone, they'll likely feel disconnected from you.

SELF-ABSORPTION BLOCKS
OUR AWARENESS OF OTHERS

When we're absorbed in our thoughts, we often miss the subtle cues that tell us what matters most to another person. We don't notice the contradiction between a friend saying, "I'm okay," and his or her distressed face or body language. We miss the hurt in our spouse's voice when he or she tell us, "Yes, everything at the office is fine." We fail to notice the disappointment in our teenager's face when he didn't get invited to a party. Engrossed in thought, we miss the here-and-now moments that give us the opportunity to understand what others are feeling and make them and ourselves feel loved.

Our beautiful minds are treasures, but they can also undermine our health and isolate us from others. Among the habits of the mind that cause us the greatest physical and emotional problems is worry.

WORRY LOOKS FOR ANSWERS AND PROTECTION IN THE WRONG PLACES

With help from the media that relentlessly exposes us to sensational and frightening possibilities, worry is practically a global pastime. In fact, worry is so common that you almost expect it to be hereditary. But it isn't. Families pass the habit of worrying from one generation to the next not through DNA, but through example. When you grow up seeing your parents with wrinkled brows, withdrawn, and deep in thought, you get the message: When things aren't good, think extra hard about them.

Worrying, it seems, is how to solve problems, how to avoid making mistakes, how to avoid surprises, and how to be responsible. There is little evidence to support these conclusions, but the habit is so familiar that we accept it. As Mark's story illustrates, few of us are aware of the way worry shuts down our ability to make others feel loved.

The man who worried to try and keep control

Mark married Julia expecting their love for one another to last a lifetime, but unfortunately it didn't. Even with the birth of their two daughters and the effort each of them put into parenting, they grew apart. Fifteen years into the marriage, Mark discovered that Julia was having an affair. Rather than breaking up his family, Mark decided to forgive Julia and give their marriage a fresh start. But when the relationship between Julia and their teenagers became an unending war zone, and when he discovered a second infidelity on Julia's part, he filed for divorce. Julia contested the divorce and employed lawyer after a lawyer in an effort to oppose Mark's wishes and make his life as miserable as possible. Nothing he could say or do motivated her to put her rage aside. The angrier and more litigious she got, the more Mark sought refuge in his thoughts. The more uncertain life became, the more he worried.

As a child, Mark spent a lot of time alone in his room fantasizing. When he was hurting, he retreated into what seemed like a safe space. It was more comfortable for Mark to think about what had happened, and to theorize as to why it happened, than to actually feel his heartbreak. What had he done to elicit so much rage from Julia? Why didn't she see how hard he had tried to make their life together work? Would his life ever be normal again? The more out of control he felt, the more Mark tried to gain control by anxiously problem solving, planning, and strategizing. What he did most, however, was worry.

Mark worried about what was happening to his children. He worried about finances and what would become of his business if Julia took all his money. Day and night, he worried about things that had happened or could happen. The more he turned thoughts to anxious possibilities, the more stressed he became. Anxiety, and the sleeplessness that accompanied it, exhausted Mark physically and muddied his ability to think clearly and constructively. The close relationship with his children began to unravel as he became less attentive and they became more needy.

What Mark feared most began to happen as he made a series of bad decisions. In the past he had the patience and presence of mind to successfully resolve differences with his kids. Now, exhausted and fearful, he couldn't set aside his point of view to see theirs. It seemed to Mark that he was losing everything that mattered to him.

Of course, there is nothing wrong with spending time alone with our thoughts. Some of the greatest human achievements were conceived this way. However, the quality of our thinking is shaped by what we do or do not feel. Thoughts inspired by an excitement for something produce a much different product than thoughts motivated by fear. If we come to a task because we are excited and happy about it, odds are that our experience will be positive. When we are apprehensive and worried, we are far less likely to succeed.

WORRY CHANGES THE BRAIN

Experience changes the brain. This includes internal experiences that we create with our thoughts. From the brain's perspective, absorbing internal experiences can have as much as, or more influence than, external experiences. When we get lost in our thoughts because we don't like what we're feeling, anxiety and increased stress shape our thinking process. Going over the same unpleasant thing again and again in our heads is an exhausting experience that invites overwhelming stress. Worrying is stressful. It creates a situation where we think neither wisely nor well. Relentless anxiety and lack of sleep leave us angry and withdrawn, and we can shut down entirely.

Unless it's a matter of life or death, decisions made from a place of fear are rarely good decisions. Most decisions are not about fight or flight, but rather help us simply get on with our lives. When our goal is to make life better, worry gets in the way of what we need.

Negative thought habits, however, are not limited to worrying and multitasking. Making up our minds in advance, or prejudging situations or people, is another stumbling block that gets in the way of our need to feel loved.

MADE UP IN THE MIND

Solitude is a choice that many people enjoy, but not loneliness. A world in which we feel disconnected from others is an unsafe, unfriendly place, and remains so even when the disconnection is of our own making. Many people create an inner world of isolation and disconnection by remaining in their thoughts while they interact with others. When we attempt to listen while absorbed in thought, we are only listening to ourselves.

WE CAN GET THE TUNE WRONG IF WE ONLY LISTEN TO OUR OWN MELODY

In a world composed of our own thoughts, our reasoning goes unchallenged. A desire to hold on to the familiar can narrow our perspective and make us cling to preconceived ideas. Alone, we can make the known, the presumed, the predigested, and the uncontested the basis of our ideas and opinions. When this happens, our desire for the familiar can lead us down a fool's path. For example, if I've convinced myself that I am only interested in people who dress or act in a particular way, I'm going to miss many opportunities to get to know people I might like a lot. Rigid adherence to what we feel comfortable knowing can turn us into faulty thinkers. From here it is an easy step to dogmatic thinking, where we make up our minds in advance of our experience. Without a mindset that remains open to new people, ideas, options, and possibilities, we get stuck in the revolving door of our own opinions.

WHY WE GET STUCK IN OUR HEADS

Bad habits of the mind begin for many reasons. If the people who surrounded us as we grew up were preoccupied by their thoughts and making up their minds in advance of experience, then it's likely we learned by example to retreat into our minds. Educational experiences may also have encouraged us to believe that learning is a solitary, internal experience. Resistance to change is another reason we stay inside our heads.

Rapid change is a common aspect of modern life. Not only do large parts of our lives often change, but so do the small parts. For example, just as we grow comfortable with a familiar piece of technology, it changes. So do our favorite stores, brands, and restaurants. Loss of the familiar prompts us to look for protection in the confines of our thoughts. Inside the presumed safety of our mental processes, we can construct a world of our choosing—a world that doesn't have to change. As life grows increasingly unpredictable, our thoughts become a lifeline to the familiar. But when we spend too much time exclusively in our own thoughts, we miss opportunities to discover other experiences, ideas, and people, as well as chances to feel loved.

IF ALL WE DO IS THINK,
ARE WE REALLY BEING SMART?

Is intelligence simply a matter of thought? Apparently not; an ever-growing body of research equates intelligence with much more than what we simply think. In addition to intelligence quotient (I.Q.), the ability to think effectively depends on good social and emotional choices, or *emotional intelligence*.

HOW SMART IS IT TO AVOID FEELING?

By living exclusively in our heads, we connect to our intellect but disconnect from other equally important parts of ourselves. Unless what we're thinking about is purely abstract, we are not bringing our best resources to a problem or decision. In addition to reasoning, we need to engage the emotional parts of our brain to be our most intelligent.

We can delude ourselves into thinking that good planning and strategizing is all we need to get everything we want. We can imagine our lives so well planned that we don't have to consider improbabilities; we can picture a life of no surprises. But we can only do this by staying in an intellectual world that has a limited view of what is happening. Individuals like Jerry in the story that follows plan their entire lives before they begin living them—with disastrous results.

Stuck in his mind for love

Jerry was a very bright guy, graduating at the top of his high school class and later receiving a full scholarship in chemistry to a prestigious college. The only child of immigrant parents, he spent much of his life alone thinking things out. Jerry believed that his ability to analyze and plan was all he needed to make good decisions, so that's all he relied on.

The most important decisions in Jerry's life—including his career choice and his choice of a wife—were planned in advance. For example, Jerry's great love was chemistry, but he changed his major to medicine because he thought there was more prestige and money in being a medical doctor. Similarly, the main love in his personal life was a lovely young woman named Wendy, with whom Jerry grew up. She was very fond of him, and he was fond of her, but she didn't fit into the plans he had in mind for a wife. Instead, Jerry saw himself with Sharon, who fit the picture Jerry painted of the glamorous, witty woman he believed he should marry. He also liked the envy he saw in the eyes of other men when Sharon was on his arm.

Jerry hadn't given much thought to how he felt about Sharon or how she felt about him. Sharon *seemed* to like him. She was very intelligent and he thought they would probably produce intelligent kids, and that was enough to convince Jerry that he should propose to her. She accepted, and Jerry was excited.

In his third year of medical school, however, Jerry suddenly realized that he didn't really like being a medical doctor. He then changed his specialty to psychiatry, but found he wasn't all that happy with psychiatry, either. Also, his marriage to Sharon hadn't turned out as expected. When he was dating Sharon, her free spirit made her seem modern. Once they were married, he found her many interests frivolous and her behavior unpredictable. Jerry did his best to rein Sharon in, but

this only made her resentful. They tried marriage counseling, but it didn't help. While Jerry was willing to talk
about their problems, he wasn't willing to let down his
intellectual guard and empathize with Sharon's emotional needs. They eventually divorced.

TO BE SMART WE HAVE TO REMAIN UNCERTAIN

The biggest problem with planning and strategizing, especially when we don't take emotions into consideration, is
that the process is invariably flawed. Rooted in our own
thoughts, we are cut off from experiences that can show us
how we actually feel. We can make an intellectual guess, but
that's all it will be. Moreover, if we're deep in thought, we
won't receive the emotional messages sent by others that tell
us we are loved. Neither will we be able to provide others
with the connections they need to feel loved.

Ironically, our most important thoughts often come to
us when we're not thinking with a specific purpose, or when
we least expect them. They come to us in dreams, in the
shower, while we are rock climbing or lying in the grass staring at the stars. Our most important thoughts come to us;
we don't need to go to them. They come to us when we are
calm, focused, safe, relaxed, and as much aware of what we
feel as what we think.

Part III

TOOLS FOR REPLACING
STRESS WITH LOVE

Once you identify the kind of experience you need in order to feel loved and recognize the obstacles you create that stifle these needs, you are ready for change. And behavioral change is possible because, as we now know, our brains are capable of change for the better throughout life. We also know how brain change occurs: when new learning is consistently practiced over time.

With this in mind, you are at the point in the book of acquiring new skills that will enable you to feel loved, even when you're overwhelmed by stress. You are ready to learn skills that are powerful enough to keep threatening experiences from becoming events where fear and instinct crush your possibilities for feeling loved.

Part Three of Feeling Loved *first examines the kind of skills needed to replace stress with love. These skills emulate the brain developments that occur in newborns when they have connected, secure relationships with their caretakers. Part Three will also introduce you to a toolkit that contains a step-by-step process for learning these skills.*

CHAPTER 6

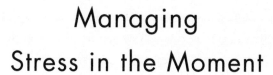

Managing
Stress in the Moment

As the earlier chapters have shown, stress has a great deal to do with why we don't feel loved or aren't able to make those we care about feel loved. Think of stress in much the same way as you think of body temperature: Both temperature and stress are states of balance within the body. In order for us to feel and be our best, each needs to be neither too high nor too low. When we are outside a functional range of stress, or a "zone of well-being," we are unlikely to make wise decisions, resolve challenging issues, or make meaningful connections with others.

Stress is an efficient state of balance that was easy to recognize when the threats we faced were largely external. However, the world we now live in poses challenges that have more to do with the *perception* of danger and anxiety than the actual *presence* of imminent danger.

THREATS TO SAFETY ARE INTERNAL AS WELL AS EXTERNAL

Our nervous systems have developed over the past 100,000 years or more. In the beginning, humans lived in the wild, where they were threatened by starvation, exposure, and predators. Danger was imminent but not always present. In such a world, our nervous systems functioned well. In the face of impending danger, we instinctively fought, ran for our lives, or played dead. These strategies worked enough times to preserve the existence of human life. But today we live in a very different world, where things that threaten us are not necessarily immediate and may not threaten our physical well-being.

We now face stressors that often are more internal than external. Day in and day out, work and personal life challenges routinely create stress imbalances. Modern-day stressors are often responses to the unknown, to a psychologically threatening change rather than an immediate, life-threatening possibility. What lies ahead, what could or might be, what we have lost, or what we may uncover are all thoughts that pose a greater threat to our psyches than they do to our lives.

Modern life is hardly free from disaster, but on the whole we live more in anticipation of disaster than in dealing with it. The anticipatory fear that characterizes the human stress response is called anxiety, and it's as much of a stressor as fear itself. Anxiety is a common emotional stressor that can play havoc with our lives.

BOTH TOO MUCH AND TOO LITTLE STRESS CAN UNDERMINE OUR RELATIONSHIPS

Though the role of stress is to preserve life, the complexities of modern life have changed the amount of stress we can endure and the way in which we respond to stress. Our multitasking and access to smartphones mean we're expected to always be available, always connected and responding. Without a break, we allow hundreds of small day-to-day stressors to trigger automatic responses that were once reserved only for immediate threats to our lives. Yes, some of the stressors we face daily are psychologically and emotionally threatening, but they're not life-threatening. Our nervous systems are now confused and out of balance with too much unhealthy stress. And the body's natural, reflexive response to stress is no longer appropriate for all of these less-immediate threats. Fight, flight, or freeze isn't a suitable response to an urgent text from your boss or spouse, for example. In fact, these automatic reactions often shut down our ability to feel loved and make others feel loved.

It's important to recognize reflexive responses to stressors, but you won't be able to do this if you don't recognize what healthy stress actually feels like. When stress lies within a healthy, acceptable range, you are energized, alert, focused, calm, and relaxed. I call this desirable stress region the "E-Zone." When we find ourselves in it, we are energized, efficient, and at ease. When we feel threatened, however, we disconnect from this stable E-Zone stress region. Even when the threat is only theoretical, we can move out of the E-Zone and become at risk for hurtful and self-defeating actions, as the following stories depict.

Examples of people who suffered stress outside of their E-Zone

Before they were married, **Ray** and **Denise** spent hours listening and talking to one another. Denise's ability to give Ray her rapt attention was what first attracted him to her; he had never met anyone so eager to understand his feelings. The more she listened, the more deeply he fell in love. Their first years together were happy and relaxed, but the stressors at work and the demands of a growing family began adding stress to their lives. Drained by the day's challenges, they looked to one another for nurturing but were both too overwhelmed to provide it. This loss closed the door on a very important part of their relationship and added further stress to their lives. Ray, to feel more relaxed, began stopping at a local bar for drinks and conversation before heading home. Denise became increasingly angry and withdrawn, rarely speaking to or even looking at Ray.

Angela was an attractive and talented dancer who couldn't seem to get a job. Time and again she tried out for roles she believed were just right for her. When she walked out of the room, she felt good about her audition and thought the choreographer was impressed. However, she never got a call back. She told friends and family that at the age of thirty she was too old for the dance world. But age wasn't the problem. Angela coped with her performance anxiety by talking incessantly—even when others were auditioning. Not surprisingly, this upset the choreographer and other dancers. It was her nonstop chatter, fanned by anxiety, that created resentment and made others overlook her talents.

Connie was thrilled when she met Rick, who, like herself, was a devoted single parent with young children. The two of them seemed to have so much in common, sharing the same values and enjoying the same activities. When Rick invited Connie to a family gathering, she was both thrilled and very nervous. Connie knew that Rick was close to his mother, and she wanted to be relaxed and make a good impression. To calm down, she had a drink before the party and a few more during dinner to ease her nervousness. But this way of coping with the threatening presence of Rick's mother only made matters worse. Connie wasn't used to drinking and became very drunk. Rick's mom, thinking Connie was an alcoholic, warned her son about getting involved with her.

Many people are out of touch with the emotional and psychological stressors that automatically throw them off balance. Non-life-threatening, day-to-day stress drains our energy, clouds our thinking, and makes it harder to have fulfilling relationships.

SUCCESSFUL RELATIONSHIPS
REQUIRE US TO STAY IN THE E-ZONE

If we're angry, withdrawn, or spaced out, we're not in a position to communicate well, behave with sensitivity, or think clearly. When in survival mode, we are also likely to be self-centered and self-absorbed, reacting strongly to small details that only slightly impact our lives. It's not that we're bad people or don't know how to act; we simply have nervous systems that automatically respond to situations we perceive as threatening, even if they aren't.

In the alarm phase—when our response to stress becomes too high or too low—we are severely limited in the way we think, feel, and act. We may overreact or underreact and say things we normally wouldn't say, or do things we wouldn't normally do. When the real or supposed danger has passed, our nervous systems automatically return to a stable range of stress, but by then it might be too late and we may have unintentionally damaged a relationship. The choices made in an unbalanced state of stress often result in hurting others and ourselves. Fortunately, we can learn responses that bring our stress levels back into the E-Zone. While we can't always control what happens to us, we can learn to control how we react to what happens. These skills enable us to take charge of our relationships and our lives.

STRESS OUTSIDE THE E-ZONE TRIGGERS A CASCADE OF EMOTIONAL PROBLEMS

It's not uncommon for someone living with stress outside the E-Zone to become anxious or depressed. Stressors that include insufficient sleep, major life changes, work problems, and family and relationship problems trigger both stress and emotional distress. Many things that appear threatening can bring unresolved emotional problems to the surface, making these emotional problems the source of additional stressors that further aggravate our problems. Though the exact biological relationship between stress and emotion remains unclear, there is an observable connection between the two. Stress pushes emotional buttons that result in self-defeating thoughts and actions. This distressing behavior directly leads to more stress, as this next story demonstrates.

The couple whose stress blocked their ability to communicate

John and **Audrey** had both been married and divorced before they met in graduate school and fell in love by helping each other with their "emotional issues." John's issues stemmed from the divorce of his adoptive parents when he was two years old, which affected his ability to feel secure, making it difficult for him to trust others. Audrey, an only child, grew up pressured by her parents' need for perfection. She stuttered as a child and remained tense as an adult. Both John and Audrey were grateful to have found excellent communicators and compassionate listeners in one another. They married, had their first child, and completed their degrees as marriage and family counselors.

The successful and attractive couple soon had a thriving practice that centered on methods of communicating that they had developed. John and Audrey had two more children and became so popular professionally that they had a long waiting list of clients. As their responsibilities and the demands on their time increased, they began feeling more pressure. Old problems from their earlier marriages resurfaced. John's old back injury started bothering him again, and he began feeling that he didn't have Audrey's attention. Hurt, John withdrew into himself. Audrey didn't understand why John was upset and responded by withdrawing, too, and became increasingly tense and angry. Under the weight of stress that never seemed to end, automatic flight-or-fight behavior began influencing their relationship. Though they continued teaching their communication methods to other people, their ability to communicate with each other was compromised.

Missing her emotional connection with John, Audrey turned to her friend, a single woman, for comfort. Talking with this friend calmed and reassured her, but little did she know that John felt threatened by the friendship. He became increasingly jealous, resentful, and even more withdrawn. His behavior increased Audrey's resentment of him and she only grew closer to her friend. Under the pain and pressure of feeling rejected, John did something very uncharacteristic of him: In the middle of a confrontation with Audrey, instead of withdrawing, he flew into a rage. The rage was so unexpected and intense that it terrified Audrey. Soon, she obtained a restraining order and refused to let John in the house. From then on, their relationship remained acrimonious until their divorce.

As successful marriage and family counselors, John and Audrey knew a great deal about communication and what it took to have a successful relationship. However, when they *themselves* felt threatened, their automatic stress responses took over and they were unable to act on what they knew.

STRESSORS DISRUPT OUR BEST INTENTIONS AND PLANS FOR GOOD RELATIONSHIPS

Strategies for creating successful relationships are good to have, but they quickly lose their power in overwhelmingly stressful or threatening situations. Even the best-laid plans become ineffective when we feel threatened. Extreme or chronic stress disables our thoughts, emotions, and actions. In the grip of the all-powerful reflex of our nervous systems, we respond in habitual ways that are hurtful and self-defeating. All of our plans and good intentions are lost as instincts for survival take us by surprise and grab control of our behavior.

When we feel threatened, it's impossible to focus on anything but our immediate need for safety. Unless we have the ability to recognize what's happening to us and quickly bring stress into balance, we will not be able to act on what we know or what we've planned. In a world where threat is less *external* and more *internal*, we need to better understand and manage stress so that it doesn't become overwhelming.

CHALLENGES TO KEEPING STRESS IN THE E-ZONE

Stress is such an accepted part of modern life that many of us believe we can recognize and understand it. Years of taking questions and comments on one of the world's largest mental health websites, Helpguide.org, makes me question this assumption. Because our modern stressors are often internal, our awareness of their influence on our thoughts and actions is often inadequate. We are apt to ignore stressors that aren't life-threatening but are nonetheless constant and disabling. As Maria's story demonstrates, it's these internal stressors that contribute to anxiety and are often the source of our relationship problems.

The woman who dealt with her stress by blaming others

Maria was bright and dedicated, but she didn't enjoy working until she got her dream job as the executive chef at a critically acclaimed restaurant. Stomach problems that plagued her in previous jobs were suddenly gone, and each day she woke up in anticipation of the challenges that lay ahead. Because her accomplishments were acknowledged in the media, Maria felt appreciated, and because the restaurant did so well, she saw two salary increases in less than two years. Then the owner hired Bruce as the sous chef.

Bruce was younger than Maria and a real dynamo. He tackled everything in the kitchen with self-assurance and inexhaustible energy, and the wait staff found him charming. Bruce didn't have Maria's experience, but his youth and energy intimidated her. She found herself making unfavorable comparisons between him and herself, and though she had no reason to believe that her boss was dissatisfied with her work, Maria began to worry about being replaced by Bruce. The more she worried, the more anxious, resentful, and withdrawn she became. Maria didn't realize her new emotions were the result of stress. She thought being stressed meant acting out, and she certainly wasn't doing that. Even when her old stomach problems returned, she didn't consider that it could have anything to do with stress.

Even though Maria didn't recognize that she was stressed, she did notice that she was not her old self at work. She began to mix up orders, and on a busy Friday night she started a grease fire that evacuated the kitchen. She began to worry more and more and felt increasingly distressed and distracted, and she internally blamed Bruce for all her mistakes. The unspoken threat he posed was the cause of her growing edginess, she thought. The more anxious Maria felt, the less attention she paid to her job and the more she feared losing her position to Bruce.

When her boss pointed out the changes in her performance, this only made her resent Bruce more. He was the source of all her problems, she thought, and so she didn't do anything to alter her thinking, behavior, or work ethic. After repeated fruitless discussions with her boss about the problem, Maria was fired and had to take a chef position at a less popular restaurant.

Maria's inability to recognize the stress she was under led her down a self-defeating path. Unaware that her fear of what *might* happen was affecting her ability to perform, she became increasingly ineffective and unproductive. Maria's story also points out how easily we can overlook unregulated stress or blame it on others. Our very human habit of affixing blame for the stress we're under is one of the main obstacles of stress management. Another obstacle is the fact that chronic stress, which is bad for our bodies, can sometimes feel good to our minds.

STRESS THAT HARMS US CAN SEEM TO FEEL GOOD

Stress that pushes us a little beyond our comfort zone can be beneficial as long as it doesn't go on too long or isn't too intense. As noted earlier, stress has many advantages, mainly in small doses. A little stress can keep us on our toes and ready to rise to a challenge. Stress can also provide a burst of energy that enables us to accomplish more and reach our goals. For instance, stress can help us meet challenges like taking a shot that could win a game, getting ready for a big interview, or taking an exam. The rush of adrenaline and other hormones that accompany the stress response often feels good.

Unfortunately, sometimes the good can also bring the bad. The short-term buzz that comes with a sudden burst of hormones during the stress response can be habit forming, and soon we seek out more and more stress to get that buzz back. Also, when we're riding a natural high from the adrenaline infusing with other hormones, we might not notice when our bodies are actually depleted and exhausted. Sooner or later, those who seek to regain these highs by inducing stress suffer consequences that are often severe.

STRESS IS TRAUMATIZING WHEN ACCOMPANIED BY HELPLESSNESS AND HOPELESSNESS

When intense or relentless stress is accompanied by hopelessness and helplessness, we often become traumatized. With parts of our nervous systems both racing and immobilized, we get stuck or frozen, unable to return to the E-Zone. The inability to regain a balanced state of equilibrium may only go on for a short period of time before the nervous system returns to its normal range, or it may continue for longer. We can remain traumatized for extended periods of time— days, weeks, months, or even years. This is more likely to happen when the trauma is shocking, or when people have been repeatedly traumatized or traumatized early in life.

I remember a terrifying dream from my childhood that I often awoke from immobilized. Unable to move, cry out, or run to my parents for comfort, I was literally frozen in terror. After a few minutes, I was able to begin moving my fingers again, then my hands and feet, and eventually my entire body. By then, however, I no longer felt terrified—just exhausted.

Any threat that leaves us feeling hopeless and helpless, such as surgery, hospitalizations, abuse, neglect, or abandonment, can be traumatizing—especially when we're young. We can also be traumatized by what happens to others. Even the perception of a threat can leave us feeling overwhelmed, impotent, and unable to relax or think clearly.

STRESS MANAGEMENT HAS TO BE RAPID WHEN WE MOST NEED IT

Stressors are here to stay. In our overly busy, overly intense lives, stress will always be present, but there are things we can do to diminish its impact. Because the brain is capable of changing itself, we can learn to detect when there's too much stress and find ways to quickly reduce it. As I've said before, it's important to remember that we can't control what happens to us, but we can control how we react to events.

STRESS DOESN'T HAVE TO LIMIT CONNECTION TO OURSELVES AND OTHERS

In today's world, we need to rapidly recognize and bring unregulated stress into balance. Eventually, human brains may evolve to the point where psychological threats won't trigger the automatic fight or flee responses. Until that time, however, we can teach ourselves to be aware of stressors as they occur from one moment to the next and develop responses that quickly enable us to bring ourselves back into balance.

We *can* teach old dogs new tricks. We can't change the automatic responses triggered under threat, but we can build new reactions to these responses. We can teach ourselves to remain aware of triggers as they begin to press our buttons. And we can learn how to rapidly return to our E-Zones.

NATURE'S TWO RAPID RESPONSES TO STRESSORS

Rapid stress recovery begins with an understanding that there are two very effective ways to quickly bring stress back into balance. To immediately feel better, you can talk to someone you trust who is calm and a good listener. Of course, that person might not always be available. When you don't have anyone to speak with, you can rely on a variety of sensory means to help reduce stress.

Sensory inputs include sights, sounds, tastes, smells, touches, and movements. Applying these sensations correctly can quickly and effectively reduce stress. But if stress overload can rapidly be reversed with these different sensory inputs, then why aren't we using our senses to do this all the time? The answer to this question is simple: Few people actually know about this possibility, and those who do haven't taken the time to explore it.

LEARNING TO RECOGNIZE AND MANAGE STRESS AS SOON AS IT OCCURS

While there are two ways to quickly bring stress into balance, there are three ways to automatically respond when you feel threatened. Characteristically we *fight*, *flee*, or *freeze*. Our responses also can vary within these choices. We may get angry sometimes (fight) but space out at other times (flee), especially if stress has triggered an old unresolved issue. If we do both at the same time, we tend to freeze. For example, if we are in the middle of the street and a car is racing toward us, we may freeze with fear though our hearts are pounding.

Internally, all three responses are alike, but each is expressed differently. The fight response often appears as anger and agitation. The flight or flee response looks like we're backing off, spacing out, or withdrawing. When we're frozen, we often look like deer caught in headlights, although this can be deceiving because it masks a very agitated internal experience.

Relaxation techniques like exercise, yoga, or meditation can reduce stress on an overall level, making it more likely that we will remain balanced throughout the day. Ratcheting down overall stress, however, won't protect us from losing our composure when we feel threatened. Though we may exercise frequently, practice yoga regularly, or meditate daily, when something threatening happens, we may still respond automatically. When taken by surprise, our relaxation practices won't necessarily keep us from limiting our thinking and actions, as the following stories demonstrate.

People who lost it under stress— even though they had coping skills

Jennifer walked her dog twice daily and regularly practiced yoga. Known for her quiet self-assurance and ability to stand up for herself, she responded to most challenges with poise. But still, there were notable exceptions that caught her off guard. For example, as a devoted mother, she often responded with shock and withdrawal when her teenage daughter became angry and talked back to her. When this happened, Jennifer became so hurt that she shut down emotionally. Both angry and withdrawn, she wasn't able to hear the real problem behind her daughter's harsh words.

Travis started each day with a long, relaxing run. An avid athlete, he was easygoing and projected confidence. Among his business associates, Travis had a reputation for strength and evenhandedness. But this wasn't always so, especially at home. With his wife, whom he loved dearly, he became flustered and overwhelmed. Attracted to the emotional drama that was part of his wife's personality, he was also intimidated by the intensity of her emotions. When faced with so much drama, Travis did not know what to do, and he often spaced out, retreating to an inner world. When this happened, his wife saw his behavior as uncaring and disinterested. She had no idea how much she meant to her husband.

Dennis meditated daily and surfed whenever he had the chance. Well-spoken and confident, he was a powerful figure in the business and political world, but he had an Achilles heel: He was quick to anger. When a colleague mentioned his chauvinistic treatment toward a subordinate, Dennis lost it. Purple with rage and hardly able to catch his breath, he couldn't do more than sputter. His overreaction embarrassed his colleague and mortified Dennis. Both of them knew that it had not been his colleague's intention to hurt Dennis's feelings, but Dennis nonetheless reacted in an extremely inappropriate way, altering their relationship.

Even daily relaxation practices don't necessarily protect us from automatic—and often problematic—responses when feeling threatened. Unless we also have a means to rapidly bring stress back into balance, we will be at risk for saying or doing things we later regret. Relaxation processes taking more than a few seconds to execute won't help rein in stress fast enough when we are taken by surprise. To better respond to threatening or overwhelming experiences, we need rapid response skills and the ability to remain emotionally self-aware.

TO STAY IN CHARGE OF OURSELVES, WE NEED AN ACTION PLAN FOR STRESS

The first step in rapidly responding to unregulated stress is to recognize that you have become less relaxed and less focused—indicating that your nervous system is out of balance. This is only likely to happen if you maintain an ongoing relationship with your internal feelings.

The second step is to identify your reaction when something threatens you:

- What exactly happens to you in the middle of a difficult or heated situation?
- Do you become angry or agitated?
- Are you experiencing an under-excited stress response like becoming depressed, withdrawn, or spaced out?
- Has your nervous system responded by freezing?
- Are you both overexcited (angry, agitated) in some ways and under-excited (depressed, withdrawn) in others?

Once you learn to identify the changes taking place in your body, which depends on your ability to remain emotionally aware, you'll be in a position to develop rapid sensory responses to stress. Learning how to rapidly respond to stress is also a prerequisite for learning a mindfulness practice that will keep you connected emotionally, even when you feel threatened or overwhelmed by stress.

IN ORDER TO CONTROL STRESS WE HAVE TO RECOGNIZE EMOTIONAL OVERLOAD

Little contributes more to chronic stress and anxiety than the stressful overload created by emotional disconnection with others and ourselves. Leading institutions now identify stress as a major source of most mental and emotional, as well as physical, problems. This is why we can't begin to address stress and anxiety without first understanding the central role our emotions—including those we most dislike—play in creating or reducing stress and anxiety.

Though we can't control our automatic responses to feeling threatened, we can learn to recognize internal, as well as external, sources of stress that push us beyond our comfort zones. When it comes to internal sources of stress, a cornerstone of this recognition is an ability to remain emotionally aware so that we can feel the changes that alert us to stress taking place in our bodies. The following chapter, Chapter 7, describes a meditative process that can strengthen our ability to do this.

CHAPTER 7

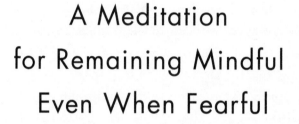

A Meditation for Remaining Mindful Even When Fearful

Many of the worst things that happen to us in life are things we do to ourselves. When we are worried, scared, threatened, and out of control, we often say and do things that sabotage our efforts to be our best, most loving selves. But here's a secret: We don't have to do this. We can avoid being our own worst enemy by learning skills that teach us how to respond differently to stress and anxiety. The most important of these skills is a meditation that helps us recognize and overcome stressful emotional overload. When we can remain calm and focused, even when we begin feeling threatened, we have a powerful means of keeping our stress under control and staying connected to feelings of love.

MEDITATION'S MANY PRACTICES

Meditation began as an ancient religious practice intended to reduce suffering and foster compassion. Over the years, other forms of meditation have taken shape, including secular practices with no religious affiliation that aim to quiet our minds, relax our bodies, and help us be more self-observant and aware.

I was taught that all meditations accomplish their goals by quieting our thoughts and narrowing our focus so that we can concentrate on a single thing or idea, one moment at a time. Our concentration can rely on a sensory experience like breathing, listening to music or sounds, or gazing at something beautiful like a flower or flickering candlelight. Some people concentrate on more active experiences like chanting and dancing, or turning around and around in a circle.

We can also focus on our internal experiences, as is the case with mindfulness meditation. Practitioners of mindfulness concentrate on each thought, emotion, or physical feeling, accepting and releasing it as it enters and leaves their consciousness from one moment to the next. But meditation, though extremely beneficial, isn't easy for many Westerners, as the following stories illustrate.

People who stopped meditating or didn't prioritize it

Seth and **Roy**—both in their thirties—were close friends since childhood. But things changed when Seth received a big promotion at work. His new job became so demanding that he rarely saw Roy anymore. From Roy's perspective, it seemed as if Seth lost interest in him and shut him out of his life. And because Roy felt hurt by this, he withdrew from Seth, making their friendship more difficult. Seth was so busy and under so much stress at work that he didn't notice how little he had seen his friend until Roy mentioned it to him. To repair their relationship, Roy suggested Seth try meditating to slow down and become more self-aware. Seth—who wanted to keep Roy as a close friend—agreed and tried several meditation practices without success. As soon as he took a few breaths and began concentrating, he would fall asleep. Instead of trying to understand why meditation made him so sleepy or why it seemed so difficult, Seth gave up. If Seth had been able to stick with the process, he might have realized just how lonely and frantic his life had become.

Josh learned early in life to avoid painful emotions by becoming a problem solver. A bright boy, solving problems came easily to him and rewarded him with attention and recognition. But what started as a way to cope with loneliness eventually grew into a habit of ignoring what he felt. Because Josh spent so little time attending to his feelings, he was often confused about his emotions and had a hard time communicating with others. At work, Josh was seen as a brilliant problem solver, but also as someone who couldn't work with others, and he found himself stuck in a dead-end job. To make matters worse, he had no close friends and lived alone. One day, a coworker suggested Josh join him in a noontime meditation class. Josh gave it a shot, but the practice made him feel uncomfortably emotional, and so he never attended another class. Had Josh been able to stick with the meditation, he might have discovered the insight he needed to improve his life.

Reese worked nonstop. She knew she was stressed and tried mindfulness meditation, but while she enjoyed it and saw its benefits, she never made it a priority. Weeks went by, and instead of slowing down and meditating, Reese spent more time at the office. It wasn't long before she began making a number of mistakes at work and everything seemed to fall apart. Reese realized that the poor choices she was making might have been avoided by slowing down. What Reese didn't realize was that she had reached a point of exhaustion, where she had lost touch with both her emotions and the instincts that protected her from making poor decisions. Meditation—as it allows us to become more aware of our thoughts and feelings—could have helped Reese see that she wasn't functioning at her best.

Were Seth, Josh, or Reese asked to put aside time on a regular basis to concentrate on their feelings, they would probably say that they'd already tried that, without success. Besides, they might say, they don't really have the time to meditate. They might even say that getting in touch with their feelings could hinder their productivity. Slowing down on a regular basis to focus on something potentially difficult or unpleasant hardly seems like a good idea when your plate is full. This may sound logical to these three—and to many other people—but it isn't the case. We don't have to stop thinking or become less productive in order to be aware of what we are feeling, provided that we know how to comfortably experience all our emotions.

LIKE AND UNLIKE A MINDFULNESS MEDITATION

Ride the Wild Horse (available free of charge at Helpguide. org) is both like and unlike a mindfulness meditation. Like a mindfulness meditation, *Ride the Wild Horse* is relaxing, slows down thought processes, and concentrates on internal experiences. It focuses awareness on the flow of mental and emotional experience as it changes from one moment to the next.

Aside from quieting an overly busy mind and relaxing a tense body, *Ride the Wild Horse* has other goals. One of these is to teach practitioners to recognize a threatening feeling or trigger, and then to quickly bring stress into balance before the automatic fight/flight/freeze response takes over. Another goal is to enable practitioners to stay focused, not just while they are practicing the meditation, but throughout the day when they find themselves feeling challenged by stress.

For many of us, staying focused when we're feeling threatened or overwhelmed by stress may seem impossible. Few people know how to neutralize their automatic fight or flight responses to stress, and some can't even recognize when they're highly stressed, making it impossible to react in a productive way.

OVERWHELMING STRESS IS A BARRIER TO PRACTICING MINDFUL SELF-AWARENESS

All meditation practices, including *Ride the Wild Horse*, can be relaxing and stress-reducing when done behind closed doors or in the safe setting of a group. However, when you take what you have been practicing in a safe environment into the game of life, you can still feel threatened and become overwhelmed by stress. You might ask yourself what happened to your concentration and ability to manage stress. It's normal at first to lose your practice in the face of reality. Remember, before you ever took your car onto the highway, you first practiced on the quiet, safe streets of your neighborhood. Once you were comfortable in your neighborhood, you started navigating the busier roads, eventually gaining enough confidence to hit the highways. The *Ride the Wild Horse* meditation works the same way.

It's important to note that no meditation practice will completely stop you from becoming reactive from time to time. There are a few individuals like the Dalai Lama who seem able to experience the most extreme stressors without becoming overwhelmed, but people like him are few and far between. Most of us still will occasionally lose our composure. But if we recognize when this happens, and if we know what to do, we can respond in ways that quickly restore our equilibrium.

WHAT MAKES *RIDE THE WILD HORSE* UNIQUE?

It may sound counterproductive to those feeling emotionally out of control, but if you take a moment to recognize and sit with an overwhelming feeling—especially if it's negative—you will be better equipped to navigate your life with confidence. This is what *Ride the Wild Horse* does for you.

The meditation enables you to remain calm and focused in the face of situations that could overwhelm you or trigger a reflexive response. The emotional self-awareness that comes with this meditation helps you decide if the choices you are making are the right ones for you at that particular time.

Knowing what you feel eliminates confusion and helps you use your resources wisely. If your head is clear and you're using your resources wisely, your creativity and problem-solving abilities will thrive. Furthermore, because emotional awareness improves your understanding of others as well as of yourself, learning to remain connected to what you feel helps you stay connected to others and yourself.

IT'S IMPORTANT TO HEAR THE
MESSAGE BEFORE DISMISSING THE MESSENGER

Some meditation practices encourage releasing unpleasant emotions as soon as they are experienced. When you do this, however, you miss the opportunity to understand the emotion's message, which is often very important. If you can reduce the intensity of an emotion quickly enough and not become overwhelmed, then you can learn from a feeling before letting it go.

For example, it's common to have trouble sleeping at night because the feelings we've blunted during our busy day often surface when we crawl into bed. We can lie in bed for hours without getting any rest. But if we're aware of and tolerate our emotions as they happen throughout our day, we may be able to rest more peacefully at night. Spending time with difficult feelings—instead of waiting until bedtime to reflect on them—can also help us better understand their true meaning. It's not uncommon for emotions to change when we spend time trying to understand them. We may start out feeling sad or angry, but upon further reflection, the sad feeling can turn into fear or anger, and the angry feeling can turn into sadness or fear. Even when the final message is a painful one, we cope better by engaging more of our mental and emotional resources.

RIDE THE WILD HORSE MEDITATION TAPS INTO MORE PARTS OF THE BRAIN

When we practice a meditation like *Ride the Wild Horse*, what we are feeling becomes the main focus of our attention. Later, however, when we're out and about, our main focus switches from feeling to thinking. We continue experiencing our feelings but in a less intense and focused way. Provided we don't feel a sense of impending danger, we don't have to stop thinking in order to be aware of what we are feeling.

Once we can experience and rein in overwhelming emotions, we can make use of a larger portion of the brain—the emotional part as well as the thinking part. When this happens and we no longer fear our feelings, we'll be aware of both physical and emotional sensations when we focus intellectually. Similarly, we'll also be able to access our intellectual resources when feeling intensely emotional. The end result of thinking as we feel and feeling as we think is that we become wiser, more productive, and better able to feel loved and make others feel loved.

MEDITATING ON
DIFFICULTIES CAN MAKE US HAPPIER

When we connect with our feelings as we do in the *Ride the Wild Horse* meditation, we learn more about ourselves, and what we discover may be pleasant as well as unpleasant. To know what we feel is to know more about who we are. Our feelings tell us the truth about ourselves. Are we as happy and content as we think we are? Are we as disappointed or as dissatisfied as we believe ourselves to be? Is what we think about ourselves actually what we experience within ourselves?

What we discover about ourselves can guide us in the right direction or stop us from moving in the wrong direction. A high degree of self-awareness and self-understanding leads to decisions that enable us to feel more love in our lives. Often, what we discover during this process comes as a surprise. This is what happened to Jacqueline.

The girl who was surprised to discover how good she felt

When **Jacqueline** was four years old, shortly after immigrating to America with her family, her father died and her mother was institutionalized following a mental breakdown. Without any other family to care for her, Jacqueline was sent to an orphanage, where she remained throughout her childhood. The orphanage was well funded and Jacqueline received educational and cultural opportunities that she might not have otherwise had. These benefits, however, didn't compensate for the fact that she had no family to call her own. The staff was kind and attentive, but she never had visitors, and in her heart Jacqueline felt the weight of being alone in the world.

A bright student, Jacqueline left the orphanage and entered college on a full scholarship. In college, she met her first husband, Carl, but that marriage didn't last since Carl found her to be too sensitive and thin-skinned. Every misstep was a calamity, and an impatient Carl resented having to always walk on eggshells when he was with her. The divorce added weight to the heaviness Jacqueline felt in her chest, but she forced herself to pick up her life and go on. She went back to school and again met someone she would marry.

Jacqueline's second husband, Daniel, was a popular professor on campus. He was a little older and an exceptionally kind, patient, and easygoing man. Daniel was able to take Jacqueline's insecurities in his stride and give her the attention and understanding she always needed. Daniel showed an interest in what Jacqueline did and what she felt. He became not only her dear husband but also a mentor and the parent figure she had never known.

Daniel and Jacqueline had four children, and Jacqueline became active in campus life. But in spite of the dear family that now surrounded her, Jacqueline continued to experience the depression she had known since childhood. She tried exploring these feelings in therapy but stopped going when her therapist recommended antidepressants. Instead of filling a prescription, Jacqueline wanted to explore other possibilities, and campus life offered many opportunities for exploration. One of these opportunities was a course in mindfulness meditation that I taught.

Jacqueline had always been a conscientious student and she practiced her meditation daily, focusing on her internal experience. The *Ride the Wild Horse* meditation initially sharpened her awareness of the heaviness she was used to experiencing, but then something unexpected and surprising began to happen. The heaviness began to fade and was replaced by a lighter, pleasant sensation. Eventually, the distressing heaviness in her chest disappeared entirely and in its place was a warm, airy feeling that made her feel safe and secure.

The process of reflecting on her emotions helped Jacqueline see that she had changed as a person. By spending time focusing on the heaviness in her heart that dated back to her childhood, she became aware that something was different, something had changed. And when Jacqueline took the time to explore what had changed, she discovered an entirely new feeling that gave her pleasure rather than pain.

FEELINGS CAN CHANGE BUT UNLESS
WE'RE ATTENTIVE, WE WON'T NOTICE

Life isn't consistently what we want it to be, and Jacqueline experienced a whole range of emotions over many years. Her internal experience wasn't always rosy. Sometimes she felt warm and safe, but at other times she was uncomfortable and unhappy with herself and everyone else. Since no feeling stayed with her for very long, though, she accepted what she felt with tolerance and learned from it.

In finding the courage to focus on her lifetime of feeling hurt, Jacqueline discovered that her internal experience had changed for the better since childhood. Emotional aware-ness was no longer as painful as it had been. She also dis-covered that all of her emotions had a purpose; every bit of feeling was self-knowledge she could use to her advantage in a life that was now secure.

Her husband, Daniel, learned early in life to remain aware of his emotions and to pay attention to what others felt. This ability to understand and empathize with Jacqueline created an environment where she felt safe for the first time in her life. But had Jacqueline not recently made the effort to recognize what she felt, she might have remained stuck and attached to old memories and insecure feelings that no longer supported her experience.

Time and experience create changes in the brain and in the way we feel. When experience changes for the better, we can change for the better. If we become wiser or our lives more secure, there is an opportunity to revisit the way we feel about ourselves. Of course, we have to examine difficult and hurtful feelings as well as those that bring us joy. But the more we explore our unpleasant feelings, the more we experience the emotions that make us happy and bring us closer to ourselves and others.

PRACTICE THAT SUPPORTS SELF-AWARENESS HELPS US BE OURSELVES

The *Ride the Wild Horse* meditation helps us build the emotional muscle we need to separate what others think or want from us from what we actually need. When friends and lovers advise us one way, and we're mindful, we can separate our needs and desires from theirs and make an informed, thoughtful choice. We can consider questions such as:

- How do we really feel about what is being proposed?
- Do we feel positively or negatively about this particular suggestion or plan?
- How excited, interested, or invested are we in what is being proposed?
- How much of ourselves are we willing to invest in what is being suggested?
- How wary or threatened are we by the offer?

These questions can help us to understand and appreciate ourselves and inform our decision-making process. Such questions not only help us decipher differences but help us successfully work through these differences.

REFLECTING ON WHAT
WE FEEL BRINGS CONTENTMENT

By learning to keep stress and emotions within a comfortable range of balance, the process of self-exploration becomes more pleasurable. When we focus on our experience in the moment, we discover there are many small things about our lives that are delightful. For example, the warmth in a friend's voice, the smell of a favorite food cooking, or the tender touch of a loved one remind us that parts of life are sweet and worthwhile.

Mindful reflection conserves time and energy and releases frustration by helping us see more clearly what is—and what is not—possible. Some things in life cannot be changed. Some people are not open to doing things differently, some situations cannot be altered, some relationships cannot be repaired, and some losses are permanent. But this is not always the case. By focusing on what is possible and what we do have control over, we can also learn to accept those things we can't control. There are losses and gains in life, and life is better when we can recognize both.

THE WILD HORSE
MAKES IT EASIER TO FEEL LOVED

Loving feelings occupy a more prominent part of our lives as we stay in touch with our emotions. By learning to tolerate and understand our own feelings, it gets easier to recognize the cues telling us what others are feeling. We hear the sadness, confusion, or fear in our child's voice, and so we stop to listen with concern. We see the hurt or anger in the eyes of someone we care about, and we empathize. If we're in touch with our feelings, we are more likely to give more of ourselves to others, and if we do, we will discover there is more love in our lives than we ever thought.

The more we care for others, the more we grow to love them. We can't help ourselves; it's the way our brains work. I remember a wonderful comedy about an arrogant, self-centered man who marries a wealthy woman when he realizes he has lost his fortune. The young woman is hysterically helpless, clumsy, and inept, but she's also generous and giving. As the man begins to care for and protect her, he grows to love his wife, in spite of himself. Moreover, though he prides himself on being disagreeable and only grudgingly admits it, he feels loved. For the first time in his life, he feels fulfilled.

We suffer as much—or more—from an inability to give love to others as we do from our need to be loved. When we don't or can't love, we are less likely to survive than those who do love. Caring and doing things for others is a way of being that has helped us survive.

WE DON'T HAVE TO SIT DOWN IN ORDER TO MEDITATE

Most of us leading full lives need to slow down and transition our racing minds to a more peaceful reflection.

This doesn't necessarily mean that we have to make this a change from action to inaction. The *Ride the Wild Horse* and other meditations aren't always practiced sitting still. Meditation can be practiced while on the move and in different forms.

Although we can meditate on the go, we still need to transition from a fast-paced, technological, problem-oriented way of being to a slower, more internally layered way of being. It's like swimming from a shallow, rapidly moving stream to a much deeper body of water that flows more slowly.

Meditation that keeps us connected to what we are feeling from one moment to the next can also take the form of artistic expression, such as dancing or singing. The following story about Paula demonstrates this.

The medical student who needed to sing

I only met with a patient named **Paula** once, but I never forgot her because she was an example of how an experience can completely change when someone connects to what they feel. Paula introduced herself to me as a student at the top of her class in her last year of medical school. Even though she had come this far and done so well, she wanted to quit school. She couldn't bear the thought of continuing. For over three years, Paula had done little else than study, and she hated the thought of reading one more book, seeing one more cadaver, or sitting through one more class. Given Paula's extreme hatred of everything associated with medical school, I asked her why she had applied in the first place. Why did she think—at one point—that she wanted to be a doctor?

Paula explained how she loved kids and it had always been her dream to become a pediatrician. Throughout high school she volunteered at a children's shelter, spending every weekend trying to cheer up the kids by singing and playing her guitar. The experience had been very rewarding and filled her with a desire to help children. I asked Paula if she had continued her volunteer work during medical school.

"Oh no," she said, "I haven't been near a child in over three years. There's no time; I study night and day to keep up my grades."

"What if you studied less?" I asked. "Have you considered making time for the type of volunteer work that inspired you to become a doctor in the first place? What if, instead of devoting all your time to studying, you began singing and playing your guitar again with children who are in need of some love and attention?"

"I would probably flunk out of medical school," she said.

"What do you have to lose, given your intention to quit anyway?" I asked.

Paula agreed to think over our conversation and let me know what happened. Nearly a year later, I had just about given up hope of hearing from her when she finally called. She told me that she had resumed her volunteer work with kids and had also graduated from medical school.

"How did you do?" I asked. "Was the last year as unpleasant as the first three?"

"School wasn't hard at all," she said. "I didn't mind studying; in fact, I liked it because I felt the connection between what I was studying and the kids I played my guitar for and sang with every weekend. I was able to immerse myself in my music, if only for a short while." Paula didn't study as much or graduate at the very top of her class, but she did a lot better than she expected, good enough to get a prized internship at a prestigious children's hospital.

Meditation that turns our focus inward toward our emotions changes the way we experience things. Sometimes we discover that we don't like what we're doing, but if we question the situation, like Paula did, we may find a solution to our problem. Making the best decision is often accomplished by being aware of what we are feeling and why we are feeling that way. Many busy people rely on a transitional process to find their internal focus, but not everyone does this in a quiet, sitting fashion. Some find it through their art.

A more active focus on what we're feeling can take many forms: Playing a musical instrument, drawing, or dancing are just a few activities that can open up our awareness and dramatically alter our experience. The more intellectually focused we are, the greater our need to transition into practices that connect our heads with our hearts, as Paula did. The process is also one that can teach us some unexpected and surprisingly good things about ourselves.

RIDING YOUR FEELINGS IS
A MEDITATION YOU CAN PRACTICE ON THE GO

In a world that is so changeable and has grown too fast-paced and confusing for our hunter-gatherer brains, staying connected to what you feel is a great way to get your life back on track. It's also a means of keeping yourself focused, provided that it becomes a way of life rather than an on-again, off-again experience. Instead of feeling controlled by fate, you can take the reins and become an informed decision maker. As someone who remains aware of your internal experience, you have options that you've never had before. You can reason before you act, and wait before you say or do something you'll regret. You will know when you feel loved, when you don't, and when you are with people who can receive your love and make choices that truly fit your needs.

A meditation that keeps us in touch with what we feel throughout the day helps us make sense out of our lives. By cutting through the stressful confusion that leaves us adrift and unfulfilled in a disconnected world, we can find an anchor within ourselves. Like the tortoise with a protective shell that accompanies him everywhere, we discover a permanent resource for our safekeeping and well-being. When emotional self-awareness and the compassion it fosters becomes a habit, we have a source of wisdom and strength that brings love to our lives, for the rest of our lives.

CHAPTER 8

A Toolkit for Change

MORE THAN ANYTHING ELSE, OVERWHELMING STRESS, sparked by intense in-the-moment emotions, stands in the way of our feeling loved. Time and again experience proves this point, and yet moment-to-moment emotional stress is something we can learn to recognize and manage. With the right tools we can become self-observant and take action to reduce stress before it overwhelms us. In so doing, we not only greatly improve our physical and emotional well-being but also make feeling loved a likely possibility.

This chapter introduces two new moment-to-moment stress management tools. These tools build the skills we need to manage stress, remain emotionally aware, and stay in control of ourselves. These tools are outlined in this chapter, but they can also be accessed by linking to a free step-by-step program on the Helpguide.org website called the

Emotional Intelligence Toolkit. You can use your computer, tablet, or smartphone to access the website and toolkit.

A TOOLKIT FOR REPLACING STRESS WITH LOVE

The Helpguide.org toolkit is a road map for acquiring two basic skills. One enables you to rapidly reduce stress in the moment; the other teaches you how to remain emotionally aware and connected to your physical and emotional feelings. These two skills mirror those that newborns learn when they have primary caretakers who make them feel safe and emotionally understood before they can speak. Infants don't inherit these skills—they are learned habits. And if a newborn can learn these skills, so can you. The impact that the first tool in the toolkit, *Quick Stress Relief*, can have is best demonstrated through the following story.

THE STRESS-BUSTING PROGRAM THAT ENABLED PARENTS TO STOP SMACKING THEIR KIDS

Following a community child development conference that I coordinated in 2004, a pilot study exploring sensory stimulation as a means of quickly reducing stress was conducted. YWCA teachers and teaching assistants at a daycare and afterschool program in LA were trained to identify three stress responses in themselves and the children they supervised. Then the teachers and teaching assistants were taught sensory methods for quickly relieving the stressors they identified.

Most of the children were from hardworking, single-parent families, and thus spent long hours in the program. Some children, as young as two years old, spent up to ten hours a day away from their home and parents. By the end of the day, chaos reigned as the hungry, exhausted, overly stressed children were picked up by parents who were often overly stressed as well. Some of the children were too spaced out to even greet their parents, while others were in tears or quick to start fights with their siblings.

The pilot study introduced the children to a variety of sensory experiences with the understanding that their rapidly growing brains were especially vulnerable to stress. We trained the teachers to recognize automatic responses to stress—fight, flight, or freeze—and how most of us have a preferred response. By first learning to recognize their own reactions to stressors, the teachers were able to recognize imbalanced stress in the children they supervised. Next, we taught the teachers to use sensory input to very quickly help the children bring their overwhelming stress back into balance.

Based on their newly acquired awareness of the connection between stress reduction and sensory input, the teachers created a sensory-rich environment that offered a variety of sensory stimulation throughout the day. The walls of the school became a source of heightened pleasure as a rainbow of colors was introduced into art projects. Whenever the children rested or ate, they were urged to smell as well as taste their food, and they listened to calming music and natural sounds. The nutritious snacks the children were given became more varied in both taste and color. Some children who were about to have a meltdown were encouraged to run around the playground, while those who became too quiet were permitted to sit next to a teacher they liked. Some children began recognizing their stressors and asked for help even before teachers spotted the problem.

It wasn't long until parents began noticing dramatic changes in their children when they picked them up at the end of the day. Formerly angry and crying children were now calm, pleasant, and happy to be going home. Parents asked what was going on and were told about the study. Many asked if they, too, could receive the training, and we agreed to let them do this. Soon, the parents who received the training realized that most of the "bad" things their kids did resulted from stressors the kids didn't know how to manage. Some of the older children in the afterschool program also wanted to learn more about stress control, so we offered a weekend training course to those aged ten and older.

Nine months later, while our initial group of YWCA teachers trained a new teacher group, I interviewed the parents who had undergone the training. I asked them to be honest in telling me what, if anything, had changed as a result of what they'd learned. The answer that many gave came as a complete surprise. They said, "I stopped smacking my kids." When I asked why they changed this behavior, they answered, "Because I found something that's better at managing my child's behavior." One parent told me, "I see the difference in the way each of my kids reacts to stress.

When my ten-year-old son acts out, I have him run around the block, but when my eight-year-old daughter starts crying uncontrollably, I tell her to come sit by me for a while." The teachers videotaped their classes and reported that they saw differences in the way children behaved with one another. Most notably, former bullies were talking with, and even consoling, other children. What a dramatic change.

This training has been successfully repeated over the years with parents, grandparents, preteens, teenagers, and at-risk groups of young adults.

There are two ways to rapidly respond to stress. Previous chapters focused on the way face-to-face conversation with someone we trust can be effective. But we can't always count on another person being there for us 24/7; we have to be able to quickly bring stress back into balance when we're alone. Like the parents, teachers, and children in the preceding story, we too can recognize how we respond to stress and then engage our senses to bring it into balance.

WE ALL POSSESS A MEANS ON OUR OWN FOR QUICKLY REDUCING STRESS IN THE MOMENT

We need to be able to reduce excessive stress on our own and do it rapidly. There are many excellent stress reduction techniques out there, but most of them require an investment in time that goes beyond the few seconds we have between the awareness that stress is about to leave our comfort zone and the automatic response we experience when feeling threatened. Automatic responses to threats—real or imagined—require a rapid response. We won't be able to stop and do yoga or run around the block when we find ourselves in a face-to-face confrontation with a friend, colleague, or loved one. Fortunately, there are things we can do.

Our sensory preferences, when we are attuned to them, can instantly calm and focus us. When people especially attuned to sounds hear a favorite song or particular melody, they will instantly calm down. Others who are especially sensitive to the way things look will see a special color, picture, or scene and instantly relax, while those most sensitive to touch will feel something soothing and immediately feel calmer.

QUICK STRESS RELIEF IS A RAPID RESPONSE TO STRESS THAT WE CAN INITIATE

The most rapid response to stress will always be a trusted face that looks at you with kindness and love, but a close second will be something you hear, see, touch, feel, smell, or taste, or movement that instantly begins to calm and soothe you. A few examples could include: pressing your palms in a certain place and feeling the tactile sensation, looking upward and taking in the serene sky, touching and smelling a plant or flower that is near you, closing your eyes and listening to the hum of cars driving by or the background chatter of conversation, sucking on a mint and focusing on the flavor, or rocking in a rocking chair.

Remembering what you did as a young child to settle yourself is often a good place to begin exploring. And when you find a sensation that both calms and energizes you, take a few seconds to let it sink in. Take a deep breath, notice how your body feels, take in the sensation, and then repeat the experience from memory with your eyes closed. For example, you may vividly remember a face, a touch, a taste, or an aroma that is strong enough to have the same effect on your nervous system as a soothing in-the-moment experience.

Sensory preferences vary widely. No two people have exactly the same nervous system, so no two people are exactly alike in their sensory preferences. This means that the sound of music, the sensation of touch, the smell of a fragrance, or a tranquilizing vision will not be the same for all people. It is up to you to explore your sensory preferences and discover those experiences that have the most penetrating effects on your nervous system.

ONE SENSORY TOOL WON'T BE ENOUGH FOR ALL OCCASIONS

When we are driving and someone behind us has their hand on the horn, when we feel lonely while surrounded by others, or when someone we love suddenly says or does something that makes us feel angry, hurt, or threatened, we need to have one or more sensory tools at our fingertips. Depending on the occasion, one tool will work better than another for rapid stress relief.

There will be other times when we're in a business meeting, talking on the phone, standing in line, or trapped in a room with people who press our emotional buttons. At such times, having only one sensory tool may not be enough to keep us relaxed and focused enough to say and do only constructive things. We need a large enough bag of sensory tools to navigate a variety of settings and challenging situations. We also need another tool to help us stay attuned to the effect our surroundings are having on us—a tool that helps us recognize and reduce social and emotional stress.

THE *RIDE THE WILD HORSE* MEDITATION IS THE SECOND TOOL IN THE TOOLKIT

Moment-to-moment emotional awareness is a birthright that you may have lost touch with for many reasons but that you can reclaim by learning how to reconnect to all your emotions.

A meditation to help you remain relaxed, focused, and emotionally aware

Ride the Wild Horse is a mindfulness meditation that can be done quietly or actively, with your eyes open or closed. The meditation begins with a relaxation process that helps you wake up feeling sensations in your body and goes on to teach you how to stay connected to your emotions.

To practice the meditation while you're moving, you will need to memorize the meditation. Then, providing you're not in danger of hurting yourself, you can practice while you're on the go. For example, you may walk slowly on an even surface or swim in a swimming pool. In both of these cases, a timer with a loud buzzer can alert you to the allotted passage of time.

Any meditation can be challenging, especially one that focuses on feeling sensations and emotions that may seem threatening. Depending on the kind of life experiences you have had, you may fear that emotions like anger or sadness may take control and overwhelm you. This is why I don't advise beginning to learn the *Ride the Wild Horse* meditation until you are familiar with Quick Stress Relief and confident in your ability to swiftly rein in stress that's making you feel uncomfortable and out of control. Emotions are a good thing, but when you're afraid, emotional experiences can be stressful. This is why it's so important to ensure that, from the beginning, your emotional exploration with *Ride the Wild Horse* is safe and manageable.

Riding your wild horse

Ride the Wild Horse begins by squeezing parts of your body, from head to toe or toe to head, in order to relax these parts and make you more aware of the feeling sensations they contain. In the intermediate meditation you begin searching for a part of your body that feels different than the other parts. The sensation that stands out can be described as stronger, more emotional, or more intense than the sensations in other parts of your body. (The sensation that stands out can also be a numbing sensation.) Once you locate this part, the deeper meditation encourages you to focus on a feeling of mild distress for approximately ten minutes. Finally, the deepest meditation focuses you on more intense feelings for an extended amount of time. You can find transcripts for all four parts of the *Ride the Wild Horse* meditation in the appendix of this book.

Interrupting thoughts may occur, but as soon as you notice them, taking a deep breath can bring your focus back to experiencing what you are sensing physically and emotionally in your body. Once you've committed the meditation to memory and can easily focus on all your physical and emotional feelings, you may also want to practice *Ride the Wild Horse* in the company of others.

If you know or suspect that you have been traumatized, you may find it more difficult to identify physical and emotional sensations in your body. This won't be a problem if you are willing to slow down and be patient with the process, frequently relying on Quick Stress Relief and practicing for shorter periods of time until you feel more comfortable. It's also helpful to receive therapeutic support as you work with the process, if you are in a position to do so.

Most new habits take two to three months to acquire, and years of consistent practice to fully assimilate, but if you practice *Ride the Wild Horse* every day for one month, you may be able to form this new habit successfully. After each session, if you have practiced correctly, you should be rewarded by feeling more sensual, emotional, energized, and alert. Almost immediately, you'll begin noticing things about yourself and others that you hadn't noticed in the past. You will start picking up nonverbal cues that alert you to both opportunities and problems in yourself and others, and you'll begin feeling more and thinking less. You will notice that your sensitivity to others has also grown.

The ride will change your life

The *Ride the Wild Horse* meditation achieves these benefits because it taps into something that you strongly feel. By focusing your energy on difficult and challenging feelings, you actually start to lessen the stressful impact of those feelings. Also, by focusing on what is emotionally or physically uncomfortable, you dissipate the stressful energy around it and take back control of the situation. This subtle process can be somewhat difficult to understand at first, but with practice, the effects of the meditation will become clear: You gain the power to tame your stressors and become more emotionally aware.

Although we are much more familiar with focusing on our thoughts than on our feelings, both processes can occur simultaneously. At first, especially while you're learning the *Ride the Wild Horse* meditation, thoughts will creep in and override your intentions to stay focused on what you feel. Later, once you're familiar with the practice, you'll begin noticing that even though you are no longer focusing on your feelings, you are, nonetheless, aware of what you feel.

As you think and plan your day-to-day activities, you will experience emotional awareness as a background presence even though you're focusing elsewhere.

It takes an enormous amount of energy to blunt our emotions. Once we are no longer afraid to experience our emotions, this energy becomes available to be used in constructive ways. When we think and feel at the same time, we are also connecting with far more brainpower than we do when we avoid our feelings. Emotional intelligence is rooted in the ability to be aware of what we feel, and *Ride the Wild Horse* has been used in many parts of the world to build emotional intelligence.

At a social and interpersonal level, the ability to know what we feel enables us to know what others are feeling as well. It gives us the capacity to be empathic (sensitive to the feelings of others) and appropriate in our responses. It is also the key that unlocks our ability to make others feel loved.

UNTIL IT'S A HABIT, IT MAY NOT BE THERE WHEN NEEDED

Practice is what integrates a new skill into our brains. What we first acquire in a matter of days can take months or years to permanently learn. To make it an ongoing part of your life, you'll need to practice on a near-daily basis until the new learning is embedded in your brain. When this doesn't happen, older, more established ways of responding that are already embedded in your brain will override the new learning.

The phrase "use it or lose it" applies to more than just muscle strength; it also applies to retaining the new mental and emotional skills we learn as adults. One of the reasons children acquire new skills so fast is that they practice what they've learned until it becomes second nature—something adults often fail to do. Adults make the mistake of thinking that understanding something means they've learned it, but that's not necessarily true. Automatic responses to feeling threatened or stressed can easily trump any new understanding that hasn't been deeply learned and integrated.

A HABIT YOU CAN RIDE AGAINST THE WIND

The *Ride the Wild Horse* meditation has been taught to many people, both individually and in large and small groups. The most unusual group to learn this meditation—because they learned so fast and thoroughly in an unsupportive culture— was a group of Japanese managers.

The traumatized managers who healed by connecting to their emotions

I was invited to create a workshop for a large Japanese company that had a group of thirty-five seasoned managers who had come to a virtual standstill in their ability to perform their duties. The company had recently downsized significantly, reducing the number of people each manager supervised. The change had traumatized the managers and they were unable to accomplish much of anything. The problem seemed related to their perception that a loss of face had occurred because of the downsizing, and was increased by the belief that emotional expression was unprofessional. I was asked to help the group reconnect to their emotions—in spite of cultural taboos—so that they could reclaim the energy and motivation that enabled them to work productively.

The workshop lasted five full days and evenings, with the final day devoted to integrating what they had learned into an inhospitable culture. In order to be successful, core beliefs and habits would have to change dramatically in this extremely short amount of time. Some things were in our favor: We would have no distractions, and each manager was very motivated to return to his former level of productivity. The head of the company also contributed to our success by publicly approving the emotional subject matter of the workshop and making sure the participants knew he valued each and every one of them.

The group spent their days learning the *Ride the Wild Horse* meditation and sharing their emotions in face-to-face sessions. Evenings were spent on creative projects that engaged their ability as manufacturing designers, so the managers could see the fruits of their emotional labors translated into an outpouring of work. The evening sessions produced remarkable examples of group creativity; some of the most impressive designs I have ever seen came out of these sessions. Encouraged by the quality of work produced at the end of the day, the men committed themselves to the process of exploring emotions many had forgotten they possessed.

In all my years as a trainer, I had never experienced a greater outpouring of raw feeling or greater empathy and support from a group. In this environment that actually applauded emotional expression, no one held back old or new anger, sadness, or joy. By the end of the fourth day, many traumatizing losses had surfaced and been replaced by feelings of safety and love. The final day of the workshop was spent developing strategies to preserve what had been learned. The workshop ended with a traditional banquet—an occasion full of mutual appreciation and the feeling of love.

Two years later, I received a call from a company representative telling me that all of the participants had successfully resumed their managerial roles. A plan, made on the final day of the workshop, brought the original group together once a month to share their feelings with one another. In addition, each member held weekly meetings with the people they supervised to discuss work-related feelings. For over two years this routine successfully preserved the dramatic changes made in the workshop.

Normally, it's very difficult for those who are uncomfortable or unfamiliar with their emotions to develop emotional awareness in a matter of days. The setting described in the story—with its lack of distractions, strong social support, and the group's extraordinary motivation—created an exceptional opportunity for learning.

A new practice can hold up even in emotionally unfriendly environments if we create regular spaces in our lives for using it. This is especially true when the new learning has social applications and we practice it with others. Our highly social brains are stimulated by social contexts.

SETTING YOURSELF UP
FOR SUCCESSFUL LEARNING

Learning a new set of skills takes effort and is not easy, especially if your energy is being sapped by depression, anxiety, or other challenges. But if you start small, with baby steps undertaken at times of the day when you have the most energy, learning a new skill can be easier than you think. Remember that change is a two-steps-forward, one-step-back process. Try to cut yourself some slack when you run into obstacles.

The skills in the toolkit draw upon resources you already possess: your senses and your emotional brain, which have been lying in reserve and waiting to be picked up and used. It's optimal if you can set aside half an hour or so each day to learn different parts of the toolkit, but ten minutes here and ten minutes there—several times a day—will also work. When practicing, turn off your cell phone, avoid substances that make you sleepy or emotionally numb, and turn up the sensory and emotional parts of your brain.

COMMUNICATING WITH OTHERS
HELPS RETAIN WHAT YOU'VE LEARNED

Face-to-face communication with others is another way of stimulating our brains and remembering what we've learned.

When we hear ourselves talking, we learn from what we have to say. When we speak with feeling, we have more impact and make a stronger impression on others. Communicating emotionally, as well as intellectually, can be a deeply therapeutic process that comforts and heals past wounds. For all these reasons, I recommend that as you practice these skills you share what you learn face-to-face with others.

Talk to anyone who can be a good listener about what you're experiencing. Be sure to engage your senses as you speak by looking into the other person's face, listening to the sound of their voice, and feeling your own emotions. Try to avoid interpreting the experience, and instead talk about what you're feeling and experiencing throughout your body. If you don't have someone you feel comfortable talking to about your meditation, write about it in a diary, as if you were talking to someone. After writing down what you would have said to another person, slowly read what you have written out loud while looking at yourself in a mirror. Journaling and talking to yourself are not meant to replace the kind of communication that's possible with another human being. But though these exercises may lack the power to make you feel loved in the way sharing with another does, they can help you retain information.

LEARNING FROM A VARIETY OF PERSPECTIVES STIMULATES BRAIN GROWTH

The Emotional Intelligence Toolkit that can be found at Helpguide.org is a free program composed of tools that offer you opportunities to watch, read, listen, and do. By engaging a variety of sensory methods, you can create an environment that increases the synaptic connections between the neurons in your brain. The lifelong plasticity of your brain permits it to form new connections that influence deep memory and permit biological change. This stimulates the potential for new emotional and social learning and speeds up the process.

Learning from a variety of perspectives requires an investment in time and energy and an ability to pace ourselves. We want to make progress, but we also need to go about the process in a leisurely way. Pausing to reflect each time we learn something new gives what we've learned time to impact our brains.

Part IV

A RECIPE

FOR PRACTICING THE

SCIENCE OF FEELING LOVED

Adults can learn new ways of feeling, thinking, and acting, but the success of the process often depends on breaking the new learning up into a small number of easy-to-remember steps. The recipe for feeling loved is inspired by research into adult learning and many years of clinical experience. "AA/CC/RR" consolidates this book's information and the sciences behind it into an easy-to-learn recipe for fostering positive relationships in challenging situations. The recipe integrates polyvagal theory, positive psychology, biological neuroscience, and emotional intelligence into a practice for relieving stress, connecting to others, and successfully solving problems that may threaten your comfort or safety.

*The six-part recipe divides into three subparts, each of which is represented by a two-letter mind jogger. The first two parts, AA, remind you to first **assess** yourself and then **assess** others by slowing down and paying attention to the emotional environment. Doing this enables the science behind feeling loved to work by fully engaging the emotional and intellectual parts of your brain. Pausing and taking time to evaluate the appropriateness of the setting, stress level, and emotional availability you and others are experiencing starts you off on secure footing. AA assessment avoids reptilian fight-or-flight reflexive responses to threatening situations that rarely help and commonly cause further disruption.*

*The next parts of the recipe are CC, to **communicate** and **connect**, which remind you to address the issue by listening* and speaking in a way that builds trust and clears up confusion. Only after you have listened and know how urgent or important the subject is to the other person are you ready to explain your point of view. With the information you have about your own needs and theirs, you can do this without losing touch with their issues—or your own. This way of communicating makes even people you disagree with feel understood and valued. By creating a safe interactive environment that activates the most evolved part of the human nervous system, mutual understanding is fostered.

The mutual trust you created in the first four parts of the feeling loved recipe will prepare you to successfully face issues and solve problems in the last parts, RR—**reframe** and **respond**. Communicating and connecting will have deepened your understanding and broadened, or reframed, your point of view. From this vantage point, you will be able to respond in a more informed, creative, and flexible manner. Few difficult problems have straightforward answers. Most solutions need tweaking to fit just right, and others may need readjusting from time to retain their usefulness. But because the solutions to relationship problems are generally less important than the process, these readjustments won't be problematic—in fact, they are likely to create more trust.

The following short chapters illustrate difficulties we can face at work, at home, and in our intimate relationships. And although these situations present a challenge, they can—when approached with behavior that reflects the feeling loved recipe, AA/CC/RR—also be occasions to learn and grow wiser. Challenges can become opportunities to not only effectively solve problems but to improve your relationships and bring fulfillment and lasting happiness into your life.

CHAPTER 9

Keeping Communication Open in Tense Work Relationships

~ A Recipe for Feeling Loved

ASSESS your stress, emotional awareness, and the setting.

ASSESS the other person's level of stress and comfort in the setting.

COMMUNICATE with questions and by listening to feelings.

CONNECT by expressing your feelings without disconnecting from the other's feelings.

REFRAME your perception of the situation.

RESPOND by acting on your revised perception.

The woman who set limits with her boss

Gillian was thrilled with her first job at a renowned social service agency, an organization that provided social services to families in need. Her coworkers were exceptionally friendly and helpful, and the head of the office, Phyllis, was well known and highly respected. Phyllis had risen rapidly to her present position despite being disabled and in a wheelchair.

Gillian found the work as challenging and interesting as she had hoped, but then something happened that almost ended her association with the agency. Gillian worked Saturdays and took Wednesdays off—an arrangement that suited Gillian because she enjoyed playing tennis and found it was easier to get a public court on a weekday. Gillian was just about to leave for her Wednesday game when she got a frantic call from a colleague at the office. A file—one that Gillian had mentioned seeing—was missing and needed immediately. The colleague begged Gillian to stop by and take a quick look around. The office was on the way to the tennis court, so Gillian agreed to run in.

Dressed in tennis clothes, she dashed into the office and began searching through the file drawer. Finally, she found the missing file just as Phyllis passed by and saw Gillian bending over the files in her very short tennis skirt. Phyllis exploded. In a voice that could shatter glass, Phyllis yelled, "How dare you come into the office dressed so unprofessionally!"

Gillian was so humiliated by the unwarranted attack that she could hardly catch her breath. Her mind was a blur and she didn't know what would come out if she said anything, so she turned around, walked out of the office, and drove to her tennis game. Hitting the ball as hard as she could helped to clear her mind. Gillian knew that although she loved her job, she couldn't work in an atmosphere where she felt disrespected. She would have to communicate this to Phyllis, but first she needed time to compose herself.

When she walked into the office early the next morning, Gillian told Phyllis that when it was convenient she needed a few uninterrupted minutes of her time. When Phyllis was ready, Gillian sat down directly across from her boss so they could look at one another face-to-face. Gillian began by asking why, even if Phyllis had cause to be upset with her, she had chosen to express her emotions in such a public way. Gillian's tone was sincere, so Phyllis felt comfortable telling her the truth. "I was just so surprised to see you bending over the files in a skirt so short I could see what you were wearing under it. Appearances are very important to me. The people we serve are often poor, and I want them to feel that real professionals are seeing them. Casual dress just isn't tolerated in this office."

Gillian took a moment to absorb what Phyllis had said before answering, "I greatly respect your views and the dress code, but I didn't come to the office yesterday to work. You may have forgotten that Wednesday is my day off. I was just about to leave for my scheduled tennis match when I got an urgent call asking me to drop by the office to help. I came in as a favor and did not deserve to be publicly humiliated for that." In a calm but determined voice, Gillian continued, "I'm here to learn and I appreciate being corrected for my mistakes. I like and respect you and love working here, but I can't do my best when I'm afraid of being yelled at and publicly humiliated."

Gillian waited patiently for Phyllis to absorb her words and the feelings of hurt and determination behind them. Phyllis remained silent for what seemed like a very long time and finally said, "I'm sorry. I didn't mean to hurt or embarrass you, and I see that I did both. No one has ever described so clearly how my anger affected them. I will do my best to avoid losing my temper with you in the future."

To her credit, Phyllis kept her word to Gillian. Occasionally, Phyllis still lost her temper in public with some of Gillian's coworkers, but she never again shouted at Gillian publicly or privately. Moreover, after this conversation, Phyllis took Gillian under her wing, giving her special attention and opportunities that she hadn't been given in the past.

So many of the hurtful things that happen in a work setting can be resolved successfully, but that rarely happens. We need to take the time and understand our feelings, listen to the other person's point of view, and communicate in an unthreatening way that brings our coworkers emotionally closer to us.

Not infrequently, when you begin by assessing a situation, you realize that you and/or the other person need to stop and wait before saying or doing anything. There is no point to beginning a conversation until everyone feels safe and relaxed enough to think clearly and be emotionally aware.

CONFRONTATION CAN BE AN OPPORTUNITY TO CONNECT AT A DEEPER LEVEL

Many of us shy away from confrontation because we believe that it can only make matters worse. But avoiding confrontation can be just as likely to drive a wedge between people.

Feelings of resentment can grow to the point of shutting down our capacity to think clearly and act appropriately. Moreover, non-threatening confrontation has the potential to make people like and respect us more. Someone who listens and with whom we can disagree often becomes a trusted peer.

CHAPTER 10

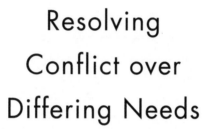

Resolving
Conflict over
Differing Needs

~ A Recipe for Feeling Loved

ASSESS your stress, emotional awareness, and the setting.

ASSESS the other person's level of stress and comfort in the setting.

COMMUNICATE with questions and by listening to feelings.

CONNECT by expressing your feelings without disconnecting from the other's feelings.

REFRAME your perception of the situation.

RESPOND by acting on your revised perception.

The couple that turned their differences into opportunities for feeling loved

Patty and **Carl** worked for a large company and spoke over the phone for years before they met face-to-face. Patty's telephone impression of Carl was that he was a jolly Santa Claus kind of a guy, and his impression of her was that she was a rather serious, unappealing woman. When they finally met at a company event, they were both shocked to see that the other was so charming and attractive. They made an entirely different impression on each other—one that ignited sparks.

There was a major difference between them, though—Carl was extroverted and Patty was introverted. This difference, however, only seemed to strengthen their attraction for one another. Carl couldn't get enough of the intense attention Patty gave him; he had never met anyone who seemed so interested in him and talked to him with such rapt attention. Her emotional intensity also fascinated him. Patty, who was naturally shy, loved the ease with which Carl approached new people and situations, and was delighted by his playful, easygoing personality.

Patty and Carl also differed in their needs for solitude. Patty liked being alone, while Carl dreaded it. Carl was an only child who grew up in a family that discouraged emotional expression. He felt lonely unless he was with others. On the other hand, Patty enjoyed playing with others as a child but also could happily entertain herself for hours. These opposing needs for solitude became problematic for Carl and Patty after the birth of their children, as Patty had less time for herself. She tried to find a few minutes of alone time before Carl came home for dinner, but when he showed up early and eager to share his day, Patty would get frustrated. This disappointed and hurt Carl, and sensing his disappointment, Patty felt guilty but also resentful for losing the quiet time she craved. Carl's response to this was to withdraw and stay later at work. Their differing needs to feel good began taking a toll on the warm connection they shared.

At first, neither Carl nor Patty talked about this problem and its effect on their relationship. Carl felt embarrassed by his need for Patty's attention and was uncomfortable talking about his feelings. Patty, seeing Carl's distress and the way it affected their relationship, continued to feel both guilty and resentful. Why did she have to give up the important time to herself in order to make him happy?

Patty loved Carl and believed that he loved her, but she greatly missed the strong connection they once had. She wondered if she needed to change for their relationship to work. Patty needed to figure out, or at least better understand, Carl's needs. She knew that exploring the emotional needs of someone unaccustomed to discussing his emotions wouldn't be easy, but she had to try. She also knew she would need to create a safe space for a conversation that Carl might find threatening.

Patty was determined to arrange a relaxed atmosphere and be in the right mindset to be a good listener. Instead of their usual Saturday night dinner out, Patty sent the children to her sister's for the night and made sure all electronic devices in the house were shut off.

Before dinner, she took a hot shower and made herself look good. When Carl came home, Patty sat down with him and initiated the conversation by asking if he felt loved. She could see that the question startled him, so she said, "I love you and I know that you love me, but do you really feel loved? Do you get the love you need from me?"

After a long pause, Carl said, "Not always."

Patty understood that she could never really know what was going on with other people until she asked them, and even then, they might not be able to tell her. With this in mind, she described how she thought Carl felt when she wasn't available to him, and then asked if she understood him correctly. "Is it true," she asked, "that you are disappointed and hurt if I don't immediately stop what I'm doing when you come home?"

"Maybe," Carl replied.

This opening gave Patty the opportunity to explain herself: "Sometimes I just need to be alone. Unless I have time to myself, I become too stressed. But I'm torn about this because I also feel bad if I disappoint you." She could see that her caring statement felt good to Carl because his face relaxed. Patty went on, "I want to understand more about how you feel. Can you tell me what it's like for you when I don't stop what I'm doing to talk to you?"

Carl's answers came slowly and tentatively: "I want to see your face light up when you see me, and when it doesn't, I guess I'm disappointed. I'm ashamed of how much I rely on your attention. I don't like to think of myself—or want you to think of me—as needy."

Patty grabbed Carl's hand. "Vulnerability isn't something I look down on," she said. "In fact, it's something I am very much attracted to. It isn't that you're not more important than whatever I'm doing, but in order for me to feel loved, I need you to understand that I need time alone to myself. I need you to respect that part of me."

Carl listened and said, "I guess I haven't really understood that until now. I want to feel loved, but I want you to feel loved, too. What can we do so that both of us get what we need?"

Making lifestyle changes that accommodated their individual needs took some thought and experimentation. By going to bed earlier and getting up before the kids were awake, they found time to sit across from one another and talk about things that were important to each of them. Patty continued to take time for herself before dinner, and when Carl came home, he played with the kids until dinner. This arrangement made their evening meals an occasion for further connection between the whole family.

Our needs for acceptance and attention may vary, but these differences don't have to undermine our relationships. When differing needs are openly addressed, they become opportunities for greater understanding and connection. And though we differ in some of our needs, we all need to feel loved.

Sometimes questions that help us assess a situation become part of the communication and connection process, as was the case when Patty asked Carl if he *felt* loved. This kind of sensitive, thought-provoking question communicates understanding and caring increasing the likelihood that a variety of successful outcomes will be possible.

COMMUNICATING OUR DIFFERENCES CAN LEAD TO GREATER EMOTIONAL CONNECTION

We are often drawn to people who differ from us because they fascinate, challenge, excite, and stimulate us. They expose us to new ideas, interests, and ways of being. They can be confounding and confusing, but they are never dull. By welcoming differences and learning to understand them, we grow in understanding and wisdom. We also gain the opportunity to bring greater love into our lives and feel more loved.

CHAPTER 11

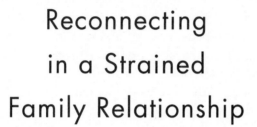

Reconnecting in a Strained Family Relationship

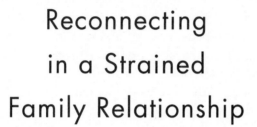

~ A Recipe for Feeling Loved

ASSESS your stress, emotional awareness, and the setting.

ASSESS the other person's level of stress and comfort in the setting.

COMMUNICATE with questions and by listening to feelings.

CONNECT by expressing your feelings without disconnecting from the other's feelings.

REFRAME your perception of the situation.

RESPOND by acting on your revised perception.

The little sister who learned to work her feelings out constructively

Lizzie and her older sister, Sandy, were close in age—so close, in fact, that for many years they were mistaken for twins, even though Sandy was fourteen months older. The two were inseparable, playing together every waking moment. But when Sandy hit puberty at thirteen, the relationship dramatically changed. Sandy suddenly no longer looked like a child, while twelve-year-old Lizzie still had the body and interests of a little girl. For the first time in their lives, the girls began arguing and fighting with one another. Their mother, Irene, noticed the change but didn't intervene, thinking it was best to give the girls time to work out their differences by themselves. Her thinking changed, however, after a particularly ugly confrontation where the sisters physically attacked one another, scratching and drawing blood.

Irene couldn't be certain, but it appeared that Lizzie was the aggressor, so she chose a time to talk about the situation when Lizzie was likely to be in a relaxed mood. Irene also chose a moment when she herself was relaxed—at lunch and after exercising and shopping for flowers. Calmly, Irene brought up the recent anger and unpleasantness between Lizzie and Sandy and said she wanted to learn why the sisters were so upset with each other. Irene wanted to understand why Lizzie frequently took many of Sandy's favorite things and why Lizzie sometimes grew so angry that she wanted to physically hurt her sister.

"Sandy is so stuck up and full of herself!" Lizzie exploded. "She doesn't want to play or be with me anymore!" Lizzie began to tear up, saying how Sandy didn't seem to want to have anything to do with her.

Irene took in Lizzie's words and the emotions behind them and asked, "Are you saying that you feel ignored by your sister?"

"Yes!" Lizzie answered. Compassionately, Irene said that it sounded like Lizzie might be missing her sister's company and that being ignored really hurt her feelings, making Lizzie want to hurt Sandy in return. Lizzie's eyes watered as her head slowly bobbed up and down in agreement.

Irene then asked Lizzie if she would be willing to tell Sandy how she felt. "I doubt she would even listen or care," Lizzie said, "but I suppose I could send her a text message."

"I'm not sure that's going to work," her mom said. "You're probably not going to get through to your sister unless you tell her face-to-face how you feel. Also, your chances of being listened to will be much better if you begin the conversation when neither of you is in a hurry and by asking her first how she feels about the fights the two of you have been having."

Things seemed to quiet down in the house after Irene spoke to Lizzie, and a few days later Irene asked Lizzie if she had a conversation with her sister. "Oh yeah, we talked," she said. "Sandy thought I actually hated her, which is crazy."

"Do you feel that your sister is paying more attention to you now?" Irene asked.

> Lizzie shrugged. "I don't know, but I'm not as angry as I was before. The thing is that I just don't think I like being with Sandy as much now as I used to."
>
> "I know," Irene said. "The people we love don't always stay the way we like; they change and we change, too."

Irene and Lizzie's story points out that the feeling loved recipe also applies to helping others resolve issues. The story is also a reminder that deeper understanding is sometimes all the resolution we need. Once the sisters were reassured of one another's love, the problems that were tearing them apart ceased to exist.

WHEN WE DON'T FEEL LOVED, WE CAN GET NASTY

Many of the hurtful things family members do and say to one another are more about the longing to feel loved than anything else. But unless we know how to manage the stress and emotions that overwhelm us when we feel upset and threatened, we will lose opportunities for communication, connection, and resolution.

WORKING IT OUT ISN'T SOMETHING
WE INSTINCTIVELY KNOW HOW TO DO

We aren't born with a skill set that automatically enables us to be socially and emotionally intelligent. If we are lucky we learn these skills early in life, but we can also learn them later on. Most family members care for one another and long to feel loved. But when we feel threatened, stress overwhelms the real issues, which are usually emotional, and creates reactive barriers that prevent us from getting or giving the love we need. The recipe for feeling loved can help restore the connection.

CHAPTER 12

Staying Connected When Memory Has Been Lost

ASSESS your stress, emotional awareness, and the setting.

ASSESS the other person's level of stress and comfort in the setting.

COMMUNICATE with questions and by listening to feelings.

CONNECT by expressing your feelings without disconnecting from the other's feelings.

REFRAME your perception of the situation.

RESPOND by acting on your revised perception.

The man who found a
way to connect in spite of loss

Melba's memory had been slipping for a long time before her husband, **Carlos**, began to take it seriously. For several years, he had told himself that his wife's forgetfulness was just part of her eccentric, lovable personality. He didn't—or didn't want to—recognize the problem. It wasn't until a policeman knocked on the door with a confused Melba, who he'd found wandering a few blocks from their home, that Carlos recognized how severe his wife's forgetfulness had become.

Carlos now saw how rapidly Melba's memory was deteriorating; she occasionally even forgot who Carlos was. Melba tried to pretend that she knew various things that she had obviously forgotten, but Carlos saw that she really didn't understand what was going on around her. Facing the fact that his wife of forty-five years had dementia—probably Alzheimer's—was the most painful thing he had ever done. Heartbroken and paralyzed with loss, Carlos tried to calm down and clear his head so he could begin making plans for their future.

Because Carlos had lost a son in the Navy, he knew the value of allowing himself to grieve about what was happening, and he let himself experience everything he felt. The ability to talk over every large and small detail of their lives was gone, and soon most of Melba's memories, including her memories of him, would also be gone. Grieving deepened this sense of loss, but it also made Carlos realize that there were parts of his wife and their life together that he might still be able to connect to. But first he had to understand more about what Melba's new life was like.

Melba couldn't tell Carlos what she was experiencing, so he did some research to better understand her sense of the world through the lens of dementia. Carlos learned that because people with dementia feel confused, this also makes them fearful and agitated. But there were some parts of Melba's experience that were not lost. She remained responsive to all kinds of sensory stimulation. Music continued to calm and soothe her, and certain colors, fragrances, and tastes continued to give her pleasure even as her memory loss became more severe. So Carlos made sure Melba frequently heard her favorite songs and music. She loved flowers—especially yellow ones—so he made it a point to place bright yellow flowers where she could see, smell, and touch them. Though conversation would grow more and more frustrating for both of them, they could still connect nonverbally through sounds, gestures, smiles, and tender touches. Moreover, because early memories would last for some time, the two of them would be able to play and sing the old songs of their youth together. This allowed Carlos to see Melba smile and even laugh.

Carlos realized that Melba's dementia created social gaps in his life that had to be filled in by others. With this in mind, he began making social dates, attending events with friends, and talking over personal problems with his children and closest friends. He missed the life he and Melba once had, but realized they could build a new kind of life together—a much simpler life, but one they could share.

Once Carlos envisioned a future he could live with, he took action and set up a caretaking schedule to ensure that even when he wasn't available, Melba would always be safe and never alone. In order to avoid becoming stressed and impatient, Carlos knew he also had to take care of himself. He arranged several labor exchanges with his neighbors in order to take daily breaks, plus he made sure to take his annual two-week fishing trip with old friends. His daughter offered to care for her mother while he was away, and he gratefully accepted her offer. Taking action made Carlos feel not only less helpless, but also more hopeful about the future. Loss is an inevitable part of life, but as long as there is life, we can feel loved and make others feel loved.

Following the feeling loved recipe may seem challenging when you need to communicate with someone you can't engage in conversation. But keep in mind that parents routinely communicate nonverbally with young children, and of course we communicate wordlessly with pets all the time. A little research into what the other person might be experiencing may give us more confidence in the process. This story also points out that even in the face of great loss, it's possible to reframe a problem and restore meaning and purpose to your life.

WE DON'T HAVE TO
THINK IN ORDER TO FEEL LOVED

Feeling loved is a sensual emotional experience that begins at birth and lasts a lifetime. Because our senses remain intact until we near the very end of life, we can continue to feel loved, provided we also feel safe. People with dementia become confused and threatened by their inability to remember and focus intellectually, but receiving loving attention can override this fear and make them feel both safe and loved.

LOVE CONTINUES AFTER LOSS

A loving connection can run very deep, especially if it has existed for years. This profound sense of closeness and communication continues even when the person no longer exists, or when parts of the person we love no longer exist. Even though we miss and grieve for what has been lost, we can still find satisfaction in the experience of loving.

Conclusion:
Feeling Loved No
Matter the Circumstances

YOU CAN BE HAPPY WITHOUT
CHANGING YOUR PHYSICAL CIRCUMSTANCES

Not everyone has the good fortune to be born with resources that make life easier. Many people are poor, unhealthy, uneducated, and lack the support of family and friends. However, because feeling loved is as much about what you give as what you have, you can still benefit from the most fundamental source of strength—your willingness to make others feel loved. What follows is the story of someone who, despite having a seemingly hopeless and empty life, created a positive change without changing her circumstances.

The woman who learned to feel loved by helping others

Carmen had one bad break after another. She grew up with a father she rarely saw and a mother who had little interest in her. Learning was a struggle for Carmen, and she dropped out of high school at sixteen. In her twenties and thirties, she had a hard time keeping a job, and her health deteriorated. Depressed, she rarely left her small apartment.

Later in life, Carmen met a man at the grocery store, and after a short courtship they were married. To her dismay, Carmen's new husband quickly started to treat her like a live-in housekeeper. But with no family or friends, few skills to make a decent living, and poor health, she didn't have many options and chose to stay in the loveless marriage.

Carmen's mental health eventually worsened to a point where she decided her only hope was to visit a nearby counseling agency. For the first time in her life, she felt safe somewhere, and for the next eight years she visited the agency once a week. Over time, the counseling sessions lapsed into a ritual where she described her empty life, which she had almost no hope or intention of improving. Carmen worked with several therapists during this time, but because there was little evidence of change or improvement, she became what the agency referred to as a "maintenance client." It was then that Carmen's case was taken over by a new employee, Yuko.

Yuko knew there wasn't much point sticking to the same approach that had been unsuccessful for eight years. She also suspected that Carmen wasn't as indifferent about her life as she appeared to be and that Carmen longed to feel loved, even though there wasn't much chance of finding love in the life she was leading. Yuko didn't know what to suggest, but she was willing to experiment to help Carmen find meaning and happiness in her life. Knowing that Carmen had plenty of time on her hands, Yuko suggested she visit a nearby volunteer agency to explore volunteer opportunities. Yuko offered to come with her for support.

The office was very small, with floor-to-ceiling drawers on the walls. The volunteer coordinator explained that the drawers contained references to more than 10,000 volunteer opportunities, and that he could supply Carmen with three volunteer opportunities at a time—as many times as she wanted—until she found a good fit. He asked Carmen if there was something she especially liked doing, and she said, "I like sewing a lot." This came as a complete surprise to Yuko. In the thick files her agency had on Carmen, there had never been a single reference to the fact that Carmen enjoyed sewing.

The volunteer coordinator then asked if there was a particular group of people that Carmen was interested in working with. Uncharacteristically, Carmen's face lit up. "I'd love to work with children, if that's possible. I like kids."

"Well then," he responded. "I think I've got just the job for you. The Crittenden Home for unwed mothers needs someone to help their girls—most of whom are young teenagers—make maternity and baby clothes."

Carmen was intrigued enough to venture out of her apartment and take a bus to the Crittenden Home. When she arrived, she found more than a dozen pregnant teen-agers and three rickety old sewing machines. Carmen identified with the girls, many of whom were scarcely more than children. Like her, they seemed scared, alone, and unloved, but they also seemed eager to do some-thing constructive with their time. Carmen was moved by their plight; they touched her heart to a degree that nothing else had in years. She agreed to come back the following week.

It didn't take long for Carmen to become attached to her students. Soon, she was using her counseling ses-sions with Yuko to discuss *their* problems. Whenever Carmen talked about her students, it was with enthusi-asm, as well as with interest and care. The stories Carmen told Yuko also made it clear that the girls were appre-ciative of Carmen and grateful for the help she offered them. "There is so much work to do," she told Yuko. "And the sewing machines aren't in good condition. They're missing parts and there isn't enough material to make the amount of clothing they need." This need for supplies prompted Carmen to begin exploring secondhand and fabric stores for parts and materials, and she was able to pick up two used sewing machines at bargain prices.

For the first time, Carmen was proud of what she was doing with her life and felt good about herself. She added another day to her volunteer schedule. When Carmen started going to the home three days a week, she apologized to Yuko, explaining that she didn't have the time for counseling anymore—there was just too much she had to do. After that, Carmen and Yuko spoke over the phone from time to time. It was during one of those conversations that Carmen proudly told her that one of the girls had named her infant daughter Karen in her honor.

Outwardly, little had changed in Carmen's life. She remained unsupported in her loveless marriage. Yet nothing about her life felt the same anymore because Carmen had found what she needed to experience: happiness and fulfillment.

Devoting yourself to making life better for others doesn't guarantee that things will always be easy for you or that you won't be hurt or quarrel with those you care about. What it does make possible, however, is the certainty that no matter what happens, your life will not be devoid of love. Visit Helpguide.org to read more about the surprising benefits of volunteering.

IT TAKES THOUGHT AND EFFORT TO FIND THE RIGHT FIT FOR WHAT YOU HAVE TO OFFER

There was a reason why the volunteer agency offered to let Carmen come back as many times as she wanted. You may need to explore several volunteer options in order to find a fulfilling fit. But rest assured, there will always be an abundance of people who need and will appreciate your loving attention. In striving to give others what they need, you often find what you most need in your own life.

WE DON'T HAVE TO LIVE HAPPILY EVER AFTER, BUT WE DO NEED TO FEEL LOVED IN ORDER TO LIVE WELL

Even at its lowest points, life can remain full of possibilities. Getting up every morning and going out into the world has always been challenging, but when you feel loved and know how to make others feel loved, life never loses its meaning or purpose.

From the stress of technology overload to the pain of dysfunctional childhoods, life's troubles are always around us. Feeling loved, however, gives us the motivation, energy, and confidence we need to move forward and make the most of what we have. In feeling loved, we gain the security and warmth we all inherently need, as well as the empowerment we require to help and comfort others. Though life may not be an easy road, it absolutely can be a meaningful and fulfilling one. Feeling loved is the key to that journey, regardless of the destination. This is the antidote to the stress of life. This is how we overcome what can crush us and instead uplift our lives to a higher and more purposeful level. Because when we feel loved and are able to help others feel loved, we tap into the source of happiness.

Appendix:
Ride the Wild Horse
Meditation Transcripts

The *Ride the Wild Horse* mindfulness meditation is part of Helpguide's Emotional Intelligence Toolkit. It teaches you how to harness and ride out intense emotions, remaining in control of the experience and in control of your behavior. Visit the toolkit online to listen and practice along with the meditation. All four audio transcripts are included below.

RIDE THE WILD HORSE BEGINNING MEDITATION

Relax to wake up

Hello. I'm Jeanne Segal, and I want to welcome you to the beginning of the *Ride the Wild Horse* mindfulness meditation.

Begin to relax by taking a slow, deep breath in and just as slowly breathing out. Take another leisurely full breath, this time paying attention to the movement in your chest and belly while you breathe in and out. Take three more slow breaths, paying attention to how much movement you can experience as you inhale deeply and exhale even more deeply.

Sit comfortably on your "sit bones" with your back and arms supported as you continue breathing deeply. Clear your mind of thoughts and focus your attention on your right hand. Slowly make a tight fist, hold . . . slowly let go, noticing the sensations in the skin, muscles, and joints in your palm, wrist, and each finger. Further relax and direct your breath to your hand and focus on the sensations you discover in your right hand.

Focus on your right arm. Gradually tighten the muscles in your upper and lower arm, hold . . . let go. Relax and direct your breath to your arm, focusing on sensations you discover in the skin, muscles, and bones of your right arm.

Focus next on your left hand. Slowly make a tight fist, hold . . . let go, noticing the sensations in the skin, muscles, and joints of your hand. Direct your breath to your left hand and focus on the sensations you discover in the palm, wrist, and each finger of your left hand.

Focus on your left arm. Gradually tighten the muscles in your upper and lower arm, hold . . . let go. Relax and imagine your breath entering and leaving your left arm, focusing on the sensations you discover in the skin, muscle, and bones of your left arm.

Next, focus on your right foot and ankle, gradually lifting up the toes of your right foot, hold . . . let go. Relax as you continue breathing and imagine your breath penetrating the muscles and bones of your relaxed right foot while you focus on the sensations you discover in your right foot and ankle.

Focus on the calf and thigh of your right leg. Squeeze your calf and thigh muscles, hold . . . let go—breathing into the skin, muscles, and bones, focusing on the sensations you discover in your right leg. Do you feel a difference between your right and left leg? The more you melt, relax, and let go, the more feeling sensation you can become aware of experiencing.

Now focus on your left foot and ankle while you gradually lift up all the toes on your left foot, hold . . . let go. Imagine your breath penetrating the muscles and bones in your left foot and ankle—melting, further relaxing as you focus on the sensations you discover in your left foot and ankle.

Focus on the calf and thigh of your left leg. Squeeze your calf and thigh muscles, hold . . . let go, breathing into the muscles and bones, focusing on the sensations you experience in your left leg.

Next, focus on your pelvis, stomach, and lower back. Slowly tighten and squeeze your pelvis, stomach, and lower back, hold . . . let go. Relax and imagine that your breath is directed into these parts, allowing your body to further dissolve, while you focus on the sensations you discover in the muscles and organs in your pelvis, stomach, and lower back.

Focus now on your chest and upper back. Tighten the muscles in your chest and upper back, hold . . . let go. Direct your breath into the muscles and organs, including your heart and lungs. Let your rib cage and back melt and relax as you focus on the sensations you discover in your chest and upper back.

Focus on your neck, the back of your head, and shoulders. Very gradually drop your head toward your chest, hold . . . and slowly lift your head up. Now, slowly raise your shoulders toward your ears, hold . . . and let your shoulders slowly drop . . . Further relaxing, imagine your breath moving through your neck and shoulders as you focus on sensations you discover.

Finally, gradually tense the back of your head and face. Include your forehead, jaw, and the muscles around your eyes, nose, and mouth. Hold . . . let go. Imagine your breath further melting and relaxing the skin and muscles in your head and face while you focus on the sensations you discover, including those in the back of your head, your jaw, forehead, and the muscles around your eyes, nose, and mouth.

Beginning Meditation

You are now going to explore the beginning meditation.

As you continue breathing fully and deeply, begin focusing on each part of your body from the toes up or head down—whichever you prefer. Pay attention to what you discover in the skin, muscles, and organs throughout your body.

If at some point the scanning process becomes emotionally unpleasant, open your eyes and employ Quick Stress Relief to bring your stress into balance before returning to the meditation. Continue slowly scanning your body, becoming aware of the feeling sensations you discover until you hear my voice again in about five minutes.

(five minutes of accompanying music)

Ending

Open your eyes wide, stand up, stamp your feet, shake your hands and arms. Focus on what I am saying to you rather than what you're feeling.

Making the shift from an internal focus to an external focus is a very important part of the process. You were paying attention to the feelings in your body—now pay attention to your surroundings. You don't have to stop feeling to do this; just stop focusing on what you're feeling and instead redirect your focused attention to the world around you.

Don't forget to talk to another person today or tomorrow about what this experience was like for you.

Finally, keep practicing this meditation until you can easily identify feeling sensations throughout your body.

RIDE THE WILD HORSE INTERMEDIATE MEDITATION

Relax to wake up

Welcome to the intermediate experience of the *Ride the Wild Horse* meditation.

Now take three slow, deep breaths, paying attention to how much movement you experience in your chest and belly as you deeply inhale and exhale even more deeply.

Sit comfortably on your sit bones, with your back and arms supported as you continue breathing deeply. Clear your mind of thoughts and focus on your right hand slowly making a tight fist, hold . . . let go. Direct your breath into your right hand, focusing on the sensations you discover in the skin, muscles, bones, and joints of your right hand.

Focus on your right arm, gradually tightening the muscles in your upper and lower arm, hold . . . let go, directing your breath into your right arm, relaxing it and focusing on the sensations you discover in the skin, muscles, and bones of your right arm.

Now focus on your left hand. Slowly make a tight fist, hold . . . let go. Breathe into your left hand, relaxing it and focusing on the sensations you discover in the skin, muscles, bones, and joints of your left hand.

Focus on your left arm, gradually tightening the muscles of your upper and lower arm, hold . . . let go, imagining your breath entering your left arm as you relax it and focus on the sensations you discover in the skin, muscles, and bones of your left arm.

Focus now on your right foot and ankle, gradually lifting all the toes of your right foot up, hold . . . let go, relax, and breathe into the sensations you discover in the muscles and bones of your right foot.

Focus on your right leg and slowly squeeze the calf and thigh muscles of your right leg, hold . . . let go. Breathe into your right leg, relaxing it and focusing on the sensations you discover in the muscles and bones of your right leg.

Now focus on your left foot and ankle, gradually lifting all the toes of your left foot up, hold . . . let go, melting and relaxing as you breathe into the sensations you discover in the muscles and bones of your left foot.

Focus on your left leg, squeezing the calf and thigh muscles, hold . . . let go. Breathe into your left leg, relaxing it and focusing on the sensations you discover in the muscles and bones in your left leg.

Focus now on your pelvis, stomach, and lower back, squeeze and hold . . . let go. Relax and breathe into the sensations you discover in the muscles and organs in your stomach, pelvis, and lower back.

Next, focus on your rib cage and upper back. Squeeze and hold . . . let go. Relax your rib cage and back as you breathe and focus on the sensations you discover in the muscles and organs in your chest . . . and upper back.

Finally, gradually tense the back of your neck, head, and face. Include your forehead, jaw, and the many muscles around your eyes, nose, and mouth, hold . . . let go, experiencing the sensations you discover in the skin and muscles in your neck, head, and face.

Intermediate Meditation

You are now going to further explore physical and emotional sensations in your body.

Continue breathing deeply and scan your body from head to toe or toe to head, whichever you prefer. As you explore, experience your moment-to-moment physical and emotional sensations.

Moving from one place in your body to another, look for a feeling sensation that is stronger or different. This area might be warmer, cooler, tighter, or more "prickly" than others. The sensation might even stand out because it's numb and lacks feeling.

This different or unusual sensation can be anywhere—your legs, stomach, shoulders, or jaw. When you locate the feeling, direct your breath into your moment-to-moment experience. Feel the sensation without thinking about it at all.

If the sensation becomes emotionally uncomfortable, open your eyes and use the sensory skills you developed **practicing** Quick Stress Relief to bring yourself back into balance, before returning to the meditation. Focus internally, looking for places in your body that hold stronger or different sensations, and continue breathing slowly and deeply until you hear my voice again in approximately nine minutes.

(nine minutes of accompanying music)

Ending

Open your eyes wide, stand up, stamp your feet, shake your hands and arms. Focus on your surroundings rather than on your internal feelings. Notice that even though you may still be sad, hurt, or angry, colors may be brighter, sounds clearer, and you may feel more energized. You're more relaxed and alert.

Distressing emotions may stay with you for a while, but they won't interfere with your life—provided that you don't think about them. Making the shift from an internal to an external focus is a very important part of the process. You were just paying attention to your feelings—now pay attention to your surroundings. You won't have to stop feeling to do this; just **stop** focusing on what you're feeling, and instead redirect your focused attention to the world around you.

Don't forget to talk to another person today or tomorrow about the experience you've just had.

Finally, keep practicing this meditation until you can comfortably identify stronger emotions or feelings that stand out in your body.

RIDE THE WILD HORSE DEEPER MEDITATION

Relax to wake up

Welcome back to a deeper experience of the *Ride the Wild Horse* mindfulness meditation.

Now take three slow, deep breaths, paying attention to how much movement you experience in your chest and belly as you deeply inhale and exhale even more deeply.

Sit comfortably on your sit bones with your back and arms supported as you continue breathing deeply. Clear your mind of thoughts and focus on your right hand, slowly making a tight fist, hold . . . let go. Direct your breath into your right hand, focusing on the sensations you discover in the skin, muscles, bones, and joints of your right hand.

Focus on your right arm, gradually tightening the muscles in your upper and lower arm, hold . . . let go, directing your breath into your right arm, relaxing it and focusing on the sensations you discover in the skin, muscles, and bones of your right arm.

Now focus on your left hand. Slowly make a tight fist, hold . . . let go. Breathe into your left hand, relaxing it and focusing on the sensations you discover in the skin, muscles, bones, and joints of your left hand.

Focus on your left arm, gradually tightening the muscles of your upper and lower arm, hold . . . let go, imagining your breath entering your left arm as you relax it and focus on the sensations you discover in the skin, muscles, and bones of your left arm.

Focus now on your right foot and ankle, gradually lifting all the toes of your right foot up, hold . . . let go, relax and breathe into the sensations you discover in the muscles and bones of your right foot.

Focus on your right leg and slowly squeeze the calf and thigh muscles of your right leg, hold . . . let go. Breathe into your right leg, relaxing it and focusing on the sensations you discover in the muscles and bones of your right leg.

Now focus on your left foot and ankle, gradually lifting all the toes of your left foot up, hold . . . let go, melting and relaxing as you breathe into the sensations you discover in the muscles and bones of your left foot.

Focus on your left leg, squeezing the calf and thigh muscles, hold . . . let go. Breathe into your left leg, relaxing it and focusing on the sensations you discover in the muscles and bones in your left leg.

Focus now on your pelvis, stomach, and lower back, squeeze and hold . . . let go. Relax and breathe into the sensations you discover in the muscles and organs in your stomach, pelvis, and lower back.

Next, focus on your rib cage and upper back. Squeeze and hold . . . let go. Relax your rib cage and back as you breathe and focus on the sensations you discover in the muscles and organs in your chest . . . and upper back.

Finally, gradually tense the back of your neck, head, and face. Include your forehead, jaw, and the many muscles around your eyes, nose, and mouth. Hold . . . let go, experiencing the sensations you discover in the skin and muscles in your neck, head, and face.

Deeper Meditation

You are now going to explore the deeper meditation.

If you are feeling mild emotional distress, focus on these feelings as your point of departure. Or you can very briefly recall a recent experience where you reacted with mild irritation. Perhaps you missed a bus or spilled a drink. Focus on feeling sensations of mild distress. Allow yourself to experience and accept these sensations.

Continue breathing slowly and deeply as you scan your body from head to toe or toe to head, whichever you prefer, allowing yourself to feel the physical and emotional sensations. Focus internally and find the place in your body with the strongest sensation. Perhaps it's your stomach, back, shoulders, or jaw. When you locate this spot, direct your breath to your moment-to-moment experience in this part of your body. Focus on the feeling, not your thoughts.

Your attention may wander, but each time this happens, gently bring it back to the place in your body that you are focusing on. Be gentle and patient with yourself, even if you become distracted again and again.

You may find it helpful to imagine that as your breath goes in and out, it's carrying the message "Permit the sensation" or "Allow the sensation."

If you begin to feel uncomfortable, open your eyes and use the sensory skills you developed practicing Quick Stress Relief to calm and focus yourself before going back to the meditation. Continue riding the experience until you hear my voice again in about fourteen minutes.

(fourteen minutes of accompanying music)

Ending

Open your eyes wide, stand up, stamp your feet, shake your hands and arms. Focus on your surroundings rather than on your internal feelings. Notice that even though you may still be sad, hurt, or angry, colors may be brighter, sounds clearer, and you may feel more energized. You're more relaxed and alert.

Distressing emotions may stay with you for a while, but they won't interfere with your life—provided that you don't think about them. Making the shift from an internal to an external focus is a very important part of the process. You were just paying attention to your feelings—now pay attention to your surroundings. You won't have to stop feeling to do this; just stop focusing on what you're feeling and redirect your attention to the world around you. There is no benefit to spending more time exclusively focusing internally.

Don't forget to talk to another person today or tomorrow about the experience you just had. And appreciate yourself for having the courage and tenacity to do this work.

Finally, keep practicing this meditation until you are completely confident of your ability to remain calm and focused in uncomfortable and mildly stressful situations.

RIDE THE WILD HORSE DEEPEST MEDITATION

Relax to wake up

Welcome back to the deepest experience of the *Ride the Wild Horse* meditation.

Take three slow, deep breaths, paying attention to how much movement you experience in your chest and belly as you deeply inhale and exhale even more deeply.

Sit comfortably on your sit bones with your back and arms supported as you continue breathing deeply. Clear your mind of thoughts and focus on your right hand, slowly making a tight fist. Hold . . . let go. Direct your breath into your right hand, focusing on the sensations you discover in the skin, muscles, bones, and joints of your right hand.

Focus on your right arm, gradually tightening the muscles in your upper and lower arm. Hold . . . let go, directing your breath into your right arm, relaxing and focusing on the sensations you discover in the skin, muscles, and bones of your right arm.

Focus now on your left hand. Slowly make a tight fist. Hold . . . let go, breathing into your left hand, relaxing it and focusing on the sensations you discover in the skin, muscles, bones, and joints of your left hand.

Focus on your left arm, gradually tightening the muscles of your upper and lower arm. Hold . . . let go, imagining your breath entering your left arm as you relax and focus on the sensations you discover in the skin, muscles, and bones of your left arm.

Focus now on your right foot and ankle, gradually lifting all the toes of your right foot up. Hold . . . let go, relax, and direct your breath into the sensations you discover in the skin, muscles, bones, and joints of your right foot.

Focus on your right leg and slowly squeeze the calf and thigh muscles of your right leg. Hold . . . let go, breathing into your right leg, relaxing it and focusing on the sensations you discover in the skin, muscles, and bones of your right leg.

Focus now on your left foot and ankle, gradually lifting all the toes of your left foot. Hold . . . let go, melting and relaxing as you direct your breath into the sensations you discover in the skin, muscles, bones, and joints of your left foot.

Focus on your left leg and, squeezing the calf and thigh muscles, hold . . . let go, breathing into your left leg, relaxing it and focusing on the sensations you discover in the skin, muscles, and bones in your left leg.

Focus now on your pelvis, stomach, and lower back. Hold . . . let go. Relax and breathe into the sensations you discover in the skin, muscles, bones, and organs in your stomach . . . pelvis . . . and lower back.

Next, focus on your rib cage and upper back. Hold . . . let go. Relax your rib cage and back as you breathe and focus on the sensations you discover in the skin, muscles, bones, and organs in your chest . . . and upper back.

Finally, gradually tense the back of your neck, head, and face. Include your forehead, jaw, and the many muscles around your eyes, nose, and mouth. Hold . . . let go, experiencing the sensations you discover in the skin, muscles, and bones in your neck . . . head . . . and face.

Deepest Meditation

You are going to explore the deepest meditation.

Continue breathing slowly and deeply. If you are feeling emotional distress, focus on these feelings for your point of departure. Or you can very briefly recall a distressing experience to prime an emotion you want to address. Scan your body for the exact spot that holds the strongest sensation. It may be any part, including your legs, stomach, chest, or face.

When you locate this spot, direct your breath into it, allowing the experience to deepen and intensify. If the feeling becomes uncomfortably strong, open your eyes and use the sensory skills you developed practicing Quick Stress Relief before continuing the meditation.

Your attention may wander, but each time this happens gently bring it back to the place in your body that feels the most intense. Be gentle and patient with yourself, even if you frequently become distracted.

If a feeling moves from one place to another, direct your attention to the part of your body with the **strongest** sensation.

If, as you approach a sensation, you go numb, experience the emptiness and let this feeling of emptiness become your focus of attention.

You may find it helpful to imagine that your breath carries the message "Permit the sensation" or "Allow the sensation." You may want to notice if a strong emotion seems familiar, if you've **felt** this way before. If you have, you may ask, "How old is this sensation? How often do I feel this way?" Don't analyze, just notice and immediately go back to focusing on your experience.

Remember, you can always open your eyes and use the sensory means you discovered practicing Quick Stress Relief to calm and center yourself before going on with the meditation.

Focus on what you're feeling internally and ride the experience until you hear my voice again in about twenty minutes.

(twenty minutes of accompanying music)

Ending

Open your eyes wide, stand up, stamp your feet, shake your hands and arms. Focus on your surroundings rather than on your internal feelings. Notice that even though you may still be sad, hurt, or angry, colors may be brighter, sounds clearer, and you may feel more energized. You're more relaxed and alert.

Distressing emotions may stay with you for a while, but they won't interfere with your life—provided that you don't think about them. Making the shift from an internal to an external focus is a very important part of the process. You were just paying attention to your feelings—now pay attention to your surroundings. You won't have to stop feeling to do this; just stop focusing on what you're feeling and redirect your attention to the world around you. There is no benefit to spending more time exclusively focusing internally.

Don't forget to talk to another person today or tomorrow about the experience you've just had. And appreciate yourself for having the courage and commitment to do this important work for your own sake and the sake of others.

Keep practicing this meditation until you are comfortable experiencing strong emotions in a variety of settings.

Bibliography

ATTACHMENT, RELATIONSHIPS, AND THE BRAIN

Anand, K. J. S. & Scalzo, F. M. (2000). "Can adverse neonatal experiences alter brain development and subsequent behavior?" *Neonatology* 77 (2), 69–82.

Campbell, A. (2008). "Attachment, aggression and affiliation: The role of oxytocin in female social behavior." *Biological Psychology* 77 (1), 1–10.

Cozolino, L. (2006). *The neuroscience of human relationships: Attachment and the developing social brain.* New York: W. W. Norton & Co.

Gerhardt, S. (2006). "Why love matters: How affection shapes a baby's brain." *Infant Observation* 9 (3), 305–9.

Graham, Y. P., Heim, C., Goodman, S. H., Miller, A. H. & Nemeroff, C. B. (1999). "The effects of neonatal stress on brain development: Implications for psychopathology." *Development and Psychopathology* 11 (3), 545–65.

Gunnar, M. R. (1998). "Quality of early care and buffering of neuroendocrine stress reactions: Potential effects on the developing human brain." *Preventive Medicine* 27 (2), 208–11.

Joseph, R. (1999). "Environmental influences on neural plasticity, the limbic system, emotional development and attachment: A review." *Child Psychiatry and Human Development* 29 (3), 189–208.

Music, G. (2010). *Nurturing natures: Attachment and children's emotional, sociocultural, and brain development.* New York: Taylor & Francis Group.

Perry, B. D., Pollard, R. A., Blakley, T. L., Baker, W. L. & Vigilante, D. (1995). "Childhood trauma, the neurobiology of adaptation, and use-dependent development of the brain: How states become traits." *Infant Mental Health Journal* 16 (4), 271–91.

Riem, M. M., van IJzendoorn, M. H., Tops, M., Boksem, M. A., Rombouts, S. A. & Bakermans-Kranenburg, M. J. (2013). "Oxytocin effects on complex brain networks are moderated by experiences of maternal love withdrawal." *European Neuropsychopharmacology* 23 (10), 1288–95.

Schore, A. N. (2000). "Attachment and the regulation of the right brain." *Attachment & Human Development* 2 (1), 23–47.

——— (2001a). "Effects of a secure attachment relationship on right brain development, affect regulation, and infant mental health." *Infant Mental Health Journal* 22 (1–2), 7–66.

——— (2001b). "The effects of early relational trauma on right brain development, affect regulation, and infant mental health." *Infant Mental Health Journal* 22 (1–2), 201–69.

——— (2002). "Dysregulation of the right brain: A fundamental mechanism of traumatic attachment and the psychopathogenesis of posttraumatic stress disorder." *Australian and New Zealand Journal of Psychiatry* 36 (1), 9–30.

——— (2005). "Back to basics: Attachment, affect regulation, and the developing right brain: Linking developmental neuroscience to pediatrics." *Pediatrics in Review* 26 (6), 204–17.

——— (2010). "Relational trauma and the developing right brain: The neurobiology of broken attachment bonds." In Tessa Baradon (Ed.), *Relational trauma in infancy: Psychoanalytic, attachment and neuropsychological contributions to parent–infant psychotherapy* (pp. 19–47). New York: Routledge/Taylor & Francis Group.

Schore, J. R. & Schore, A. N. (2008). "Modern attachment theory: The central role of affect regulation in development and treatment." *Clinical Social Work Journal* 36 (1), 9–20.

Shore, R. (1997). *Rethinking the brain: New insights into early development.* New York: Families and Work Institute.

Siegel, D. J. (1999). *The developing mind: Toward a neurobiology of interpersonal experience.* New York: Guilford Press.

———— (2001). "Toward an interpersonal neurobiology of the developing mind: Attachment relationships, 'mindsight,' and neural integration." *Infant Mental Health Journal* 22 (1–2), 67–94.

Strathearn, L., Fonagy, P., Amico, J. & Montague, P. R. (2009). "Adult attachment predicts maternal brain and oxytocin response to infant cues." *Neuropsychopharmacology* 34 (13), 2655–66.

THE SOCIAL BRAIN

Adolphs, R. (2003). "Cognitive neuroscience of human social behaviour." *Nature Reviews Neuroscience* 4 (3), 165–78.

Bartz, J. A. & Hollander, E. (2006). "The neuroscience of affiliation: Forging links between basic and clinical research on neuropeptides and social behavior." *Hormones and Behavior* 50 (4), 518–28.

Baumeister, R. F. & Leary, M. R. (1995). "The need to belong: Desire for interpersonal attachments as a fundamental human motivation." *Psychological Bulletin* 117 (3), 497.

Cacioppo, J. T., Berntson, G. G. & Waytz, A. (2010). "Social neuroscience." In I. Weiner & E. Craighead (Eds.), *Corsini Encyclopedia of Psychology, Fourth edition.* (Vol. 4., pp. 1635–6). New York: Wiley.

Cacioppo, J. T., Berntson, G. G., Sheridan, J. F. & McClintock, M. K. (2000). "Multilevel integrative analyses of human behavior:

Social neuroscience and the complementing nature of social and biological approaches." *Psychological Bulletin* 126 (6), 829.

Carter, C. S. (1998). "Neuroendocrine perspectives on social attachment and love." *Psychoneuroendocrinology* 23 (8), 779–818.

Dunbar, R. I. (1998). "The social brain hypothesis." *Evolutionary Anthropology: Issues, News, and Reviews* 6 (5), 178–90.

Fishbane, M. D. (2007). "Wired to connect: Neuroscience, relationships, and therapy." *Family Process* 46 (3), 395–412.

Goleman, D. (2006). *Social intelligence: The new science of human relationships.* New York: Random House Digital, Inc.

Link, B. G. & Phelan, J. (1995). "Social conditions as fundamental causes of disease." *Journal of Health and Social Behavior* 35, 80–94.

Marche, S. (2012). "Is Facebook making us lonely?" *The Atlantic* 309 (4), 60–69.

Panksepp, J. (1998). *Affective neuroscience: The foundations of human and animal emotions.* New York: Oxford University Press.

OXYTOCIN

Oxytocin's role as the love hormone

Burkett, J. P. & Young, L. J. (2012). "The behavioral, anatomical and pharmacological parallels between social attachment, love and addiction." *Psychopharmacology* 224 (1), 1–26.

Cariboni, A. & Ruhrberg, C. (2011). "The hormone of love attracts a partner for life." *Developmental Cell* 21 (4), 602–4.

Carter, C. S. & Porges, S. W. (2012). "The biochemistry of love: An oxytocin hypothesis." *EMBO Reports* 14 (1), 12–16.

De Boer, A., Van Buel, E. M. & Ter Horst, G. J. (2012). "Love is more than just a kiss: A neurobiological perspective on love and affection." *Neuroscience* 201, 114–24.

Ditzen, B., Schaer, M., Gabriel, B., Bodenmann, G., Ehlert, U. & Heinrichs, M. (2009). "Intranasal oxytocin increases positive communication and reduces cortisol levels during couple conflict." *Biological Psychiatry* 65 (9), 728–31.

Unkelbach, C., Guastella, A. J. & Forgas, J. P. (2008). "Oxytocin selectively facilitates recognition of positive sex and relationship words." *Psychological Science* 19 (11), 1092–94.

Wudarczyk, O. A., Earp, B. D., Guastella, A. & Savulescu, J. (2013). "Could intranasal oxytocin be used to enhance relationships? Research imperatives, clinical policy, and ethical considerations." *Current Opinion in Psychiatry* 26 (5), 474–84.

Young, L. J. (2009). "Being human: Love: Neuroscience reveals all." *Nature* 457 (7226), 148.

Oxytocin and social behavior

Campbell, A. (2008). "Attachment, aggression and affiliation: The role of oxytocin in female social behavior." *Biological Psychology* 77 (1), 1–10.

Guastella, A. J., Mitchell, P. B. & Dadds, M. R. (2008). "Oxytocin increases gaze to the eye region of human faces." *Biological Psychiatry* 63 (1), 3–5.

Guastella, A. J., Mitchell, P. B. & Mathews, F. (2008). "Oxytocin enhances the encoding of positive social memories in humans." *Biological Psychiatry* 64 (3), 256–58.

Dölen, G., Darvishzadeh, A., Huang, K. W. & Malenka, R. C. (2013). "Social reward requires coordinated activity of nucleus accumbens oxytocin and serotonin." *Nature* 501 (7466), 179–84.

Kosfeld, M., Heinrichs, M., Zak, P. J., Fischbacher, U. & Fehr, E. (2005). "Oxytocin increases trust in humans." *Nature* 435 (7042), 673–76.

Lane, A., Luminet, O., Rimé, B., de Timary, P. & Mikolajczak, M. (2012). "Oxytocin increases willingness to socially share one's emotions." *International Journal of Psychology* 48 (4), 676–81.

Mikolajczak, M., Gross, J. J., Lane, A., Corneille, O., de Timary, P. & Luminet, O. (2010). "Oxytocin makes people trusting, not gullible." *Psychological Science* 21 (8), 1072–74.

Veenema, A. H. (2013). "The oxytocin system and social behavior: Effects of sex, age, and early life stress." Paper presented at the 68th Annual Meeting of the Society for Biological Psychiatry, San Francisco, CA.

Zak, P. J., Stanton, A. A. & Ahmadi, S. (2007). "Oxytocin increases generosity in humans." *PLoS One* 2 (11), e1128.

Oxytocin, emotions, and emotional intelligence

Bartz, J. A., Zaki, J., Bolger, N., Hollander, E., Ludwig, N. N., Kolevzon, A. & Ochsner, K. N. (2010). "Oxytocin selectively improves empathic accuracy." *Psychological Science* 21 (10), 1426–28.

Cardoso, C., Ellenbogen, M. A., Serravalle, L. & Linnen, A. M. (2013). "Stress-induced negative mood moderates the relation between oxytocin administration and trust: Evidence for the 'tend-and-befriend' response to stress?" *Psychoneuroendocrinology* 38 (11), 2800–04.

Grillon, C., Krimsky, M., Charney, D. R., Vytal, K., Ernst, M. & Cornwell, B. (2012). "Oxytocin increases anxiety to unpredictable threat." *Molecular Psychiatry* 18, 958–60.

Guastella, A. J., Einfeld, S. L., Gray, K. M., Rinehart, N. J., Tonge, B. J., Lambert, T. J. & Hickie, I. B. (2010). "Intranasal oxytocin improves emotion recognition for youth with autism spectrum disorders." *Biological Psychiatry* 67 (7), 692–94.

Guzmán, Y. F., Tronson, N. C., Jovasevic, V., Sato, K., Guedea, A. L., Mizukami, H., Nishimori, K. & Radulovic, J. (2013). "Fear-enhancing effects of septal oxytocin receptors." *Nature Neuroscience* 16 (9), 1185–87.

Love, T. M. (2014). "Oxytocin, motivation and the role of dopamine." *Pharmacology, Biochemistry, and Behavior* 119 (April), 49–60.

Oxytocin and stress

Heinrichs, M., Baumgartner, T., Kirschbaum, C. & Ehlert, U. (2003). "Social support and oxytocin interact to suppress cortisol and subjective responses to psychosocial stress." *Biological Psychiatry* 54 (12), 1389–98.

Leuner, B., Caponiti, J. M. & Gould, E. (2012). "Oxytocin stimulates adult neurogenesis even under conditions of stress and elevated glucocorticoids." *Hippocampus* 22 (4), 861–68.

Olff, M., Frijling, J. L., Kubzansky, L. D., Bradley, B., Ellenbogen, M. A., Cardoso, C., Bartz, J. A., Yee, J. R. & van Zuiden, M. (2013). "The role of oxytocin in social bonding, stress regulation and mental health: An update on the moderating effects of context and interindividual differences." *Psychoneuroendocrinology* 38 (9), 1883–94.

Rodrigues, S. M., Saslow, L. R., Garcia, N., John, O. P. & Keltner, D. (2009). "Oxytocin receptor genetic variation relates to empathy and stress reactivity in humans." *Proceedings of the National Academy of Sciences* 106 (50), 21437–41.

Oxytocin, attachment, and development

Feldman, R., Weller, A., Zagoory-Sharon, O. & Levine, A. (2007). "Evidence for a neuroendocrinological foundation of human affiliation plasma oxytocin levels across pregnancy and the postpartum period predict mother-infant bonding." *Psychological Science* 18 (11), 965–70.

Fries, A. B. W., Shirtcliff, E. A. & Pollak, S. D. (2008). "Neuroendocrine dysregulation following early social deprivation in children." *Developmental Psychobiology* 50 (6), 588–99.

Riem, M. M., van IJzendoorn, M. H., Tops, M., Boksem, M. A., Rombouts, S. A. & Bakermans-Kranenburg, M. J. (2013). "Oxytocin effects on complex brain networks are moderated by experiences of maternal love withdrawal." *European Neuropsychopharmacology* 23 (10), 1288–95.

Strathearn, L., Fonagy, P., Amico, J. & Montague, P. R. (2009). "Adult attachment predicts maternal brain and oxytocin response to infant cues." *Neuropsychopharmacology* 34 (13), 2655–66.

STRESS

Stress and your emotions

Folkman, S. (2007). "The case for positive emotions in the stress process." *Anxiety, Stress & Coping* 21 (1), 3–14.

Folkman, S. & Moskowitz, J. T. (2000). "Stress, positive emotion, and coping." *Current Directions in Psychological Science* 9 (4), 115–18.

Ghosh, S., Laxmi, T. R. & Chattarji, S. (2013). "Functional connectivity from the amygdala to the hippocampus grows stronger after stress." *Journal of Neuroscience* 33 (17), 7234–44.

Lazarus, R. S. (1998). "From psychological stress to the emotions: A history of changing outlooks." *Fifty Years of the Research and Theory of RS Lazarus: An Analysis of Historical and Perennial Issues* (p. 349). New York: Psychology Press.

——— (2000). "Toward better research on stress and coping." *American Psychologist* 55 (6), 665–73.

Ong, A. D., Bergeman, C. S., Bisconti, T. L. & Wallace, K. A. (2006). "Psychological resilience, positive emotions, and successful adaptation to stress in later life." *Journal of Personality and Social Psychology* 91 (4), 730–49.

Raio, C. M., Orederu, T. A., Palazzolo, L., Shurick, A. A. & Phelps, E. A. (2013). "Cognitive emotion regulation fails the stress test." *Proceedings of the National Academy of Sciences* 110 (37), 15139–44.

Stress and mental health

Aneshensel, C. S., Phelan, J. C. & Bierman, A. (2013). *Handbook of the sociology of mental health, Second edition.* New York: Springer.

Bibliography

Bremner, J. D. (2002). *Does stress damage the brain? Understanding trauma-related disorders from a mind-body perspective.* New York: W. W. Norton & Company.

Everly, J. G. S. & Lating, J. M. (2013). *A clinical guide to the treatment of the human stress response.* New York: Springer.

Glover, V. (2011). "Annual research review: Prenatal stress and the origins of psychopathology: An evolutionary perspective." *Journal of Child Psychology and Psychiatry* 52 (4), 356–67.

Grubaugh, A. L., Zinzow, H. M., Paul, L., Egede, L. E. & Frueh, B. C. (2011). "Trauma exposure and posttraumatic stress disorder in adults with severe mental illness: A critical review." *Clinical Psychology Review* 31 (6), 883–99.

Herbert, J. (1997). "Fortnightly review. Stress, the brain, and mental illness." *BMJ: British Medical Journal* 315 (7107), 530.

Juster, R. P., Bizik, G., Picard, M., Arsenault-Lapierre, G., Sindi, S., Trepanier, L., Marin, M. F., Wan, N., Sekerovic, Z. & Lord, C. (2011). "A transdisciplinary perspective of chronic stress in relation to psychopathology throughout life span development." *Development and Psychopathology* 23 (3), 725–26.

De Kloet, E. R., Joëls, M. & Holsboer, F. (2005). "Stress and the brain: From adaptation to disease." *Nature Reviews. Neuroscience* 6 (6), 463–75.

Mazure, C. M. (Ed.) (1995). *Does stress cause psychiatric illness?* Washington D. C.: American Psychiatric Press.

Nestler, E. J. & Hyman, S. E. (2010). "Animal models of neuropsychiatric disorders." *Nature Neuroscience* 13 (10), 1161–69.

Pearlin, L. I. (1999). "Stress and mental health: A conceptual overview." In A. V. Horwitz & T. L. Scheid (Eds.), *A handbook for the study of mental health: Social contexts, theories, and systems* (pp. 161–75). New York: Cambridge University Press.

Rice, F., Harold, G. T., Boivin, J., Van den Bree, M., Hay, D. F. & Thapar, A. (2010). "The links between prenatal stress and offspring development and psychopathology: Disentangling environmental and inherited influences." *Psychological Medicine* 40 (2), 335–45.

Schwartz, S. & Meyer, I. H. (2010). "Mental health disparities research: The impact of within and between group analyses on tests of social stress hypotheses." *Social Science & Medicine* 70 (8), 1111–18.

Thoits, P. A. (2013). "Self, identity, stress, and mental health." In *Handbook of the sociology of mental health, Second edition* (pp. 357–377). New York: Springer.

Stress and anxiety

Bennett Ao, M. R. (2008). "Stress and anxiety in schizophrenia and depression: glucocorticoids, corticotropin-releasing hormone and synapse regression." *Australian and New Zealand Journal of Psychiatry* 42 (12), 995–1002.

Gerra, G., Zaimovic, A., Zambelli, U., Timpano, M., Reali, N., Bernasconi, S. & Brambilla, F. (2000). "Neuroendocrine responses to psychological stress in adolescents with anxiety disorder." *Neuropsychobiology* 42 (2), 82–92.

Heilig, M. (2004). "The NPY system in stress, anxiety and depression." *Neuropeptides* 38 (4), 213–24.

Heim, C. & Nemeroff, C. B. (2001). "The role of childhood trauma in the neurobiology of mood and anxiety disorders: preclinical and clinical studies." *Biological psychiatry* 49 (12), 1023–39.

Kikusui, T., Winslow, J. T. & Mori, Y. (2006). "Social buffering: relief from stress and anxiety." *Philosophical Transactions of the Royal Society B: Biological Sciences* 361 (1476), 2215–28.

Lapin, I. P. (2003). "Neurokynurenines (NEKY) as common neurochemical links of stress and anxiety." In Allegri et al. (Ed.), *Developments in Tryptophan and Serotonin Metabolism* (pp. 121–25). New York: Springer.

Maes, M., Song, C., Lin, A., De Jongh, R., Van Gastel, A., Kenis, G., Bosmans, E., De Meester, I., Benoy, I. & Neels, H. (1998).

"The effects of psychological stress on humans: increased production of pro-inflammatory cytokines and Th1-like response in stress-induced anxiety." *Cytokine* 10 (4), 313–18.

Mathew, S. J., Price, R. B. & Charney, D. S. (2008). "Recent advances in the neurobiology of anxiety disorders: Implications for novel therapeutics." *American Journal of Medical Genetics Part C: Seminars in medical genetics* 148 (2) 89–98.

McEwen, B. S., Eiland, L., Hunter, R. G. & Miller, M. M. (2012). "Stress and anxiety: Structural plasticity and epigenetic regulation as a consequence of stress." *Neuropharmacology* 62 (1), 3–12.

Schmidt, N. B., Lerew, D. R. & Jackson, R. J. (1997). "The role of anxiety sensitivity in the pathogenesis of panic: Prospective evaluation of spontaneous panic attacks during acute stress." *Journal of Abnormal Psychology* 106 (3) 355–64.

Shin, L. M. & Liberzon, I. (2009). "The neurocircuitry of fear, stress, and anxiety disorders." *Neuropsychopharmacology* 35 (1) 169–91.

Stress and bipolar disorder

Bender, R. E. & Alloy, L. B. (2011). "Life stress and kindling in bipolar disorder: Review of the evidence and integration with emerging biopsychosocial theories." *Clinical Psychology Review* 31 (3), 383–98.

Bender, R. E., Alloy, L. B., Sylvia, L. G., Urovsevic, S. & Abramson, L. Y. (2010). "Generation of life events in bipolar spectrum disorders: A re-examination and extension of the stress generation theory." *Journal of Clinical Psychology* 66 (9), 907–26.

Eiel Steen, N., Methlie, P., Lorentzen, S., Hope, S., Barrett, E. A., Larsson, S., Mork, E., Almas, B., Løvås, K. & Agartz, I. (2011). "Increased systemic cortisol metabolism in patients with schizophrenia and bipolar disorder: A mechanism for increased stress vulnerability?" *The Journal of Clinical Psychiatry* 72 (11), 1515–21.

Hosang, G. M., Uher, R., Keers, R., Cohen-Woods, S., Craig, I., Korszun, A., Perry, J., Tozzi, F., Muglia, P., McGuffin, P. & Farmer, A. E. (2010). "Stressful life events and the brain-derived neurotrophic factor gene in bipolar disorder." *Journal of Affective Disorders* 125 (1–3), 345–49.

Stress and depression

Anisman, H. & Zacharko, R. M. (1982). "Depression: The predisposing influence of stress." *Behavioral and Brain Sciences* 5 (1), 89–99.

Bartolomucci, A. & Leopardi, R. (2009). "Stress and depression: Preclinical research and clinical implications." *PLoS ONE* 4 (1), e4265.

Caspi, A., Sugden, K., Moffitt, T. E., Taylor, A., Craig, I. W., Harrington, H., McClay, J., Mill, J., Martin, J., Braithwaite, A. & Poulton, R. (2003). "Influence of life stress on depression: Moderation by a polymorphism in the 5-HTT gene." *Science* 301 (5631), 386–89.

Farooq, R. K., Isingrini, E., Tanti, A., Le Guisquet, A. M., Arlicot, N., Minier, F., Lemana, S., Chalona, S., Belzunga, C. & Camus, V. (2012). "Is unpredictable chronic mild stress (UCMS) a reliable model to study depression-induced neuroinflammation?" *Behavioural Brain Research* 231 (1), 130–37.

Hammen, C. (2004). "Stress and depression." *Annual Review of Clinical Psychology* 1 (1), 293–319.

Kessler, R. C. (1997). "The effects of stressful life events on depression." *Annual Review of Psychology* 48 (1), 191–214.

Kim, K. S., Kwon, H. J., Baek, I. S. & Han, P. L. (2012). "Repeated short-term (2h×14d) emotional stress induces lasting depression-like behavior in mice." *Experimental Neurobiology* 21 (1), 16–22.

Kubera, M., Obuchowicz, E., Goehler, L., Brzeszcz, J. & Maes, M. (2011). "In animal models, psychosocial stress-induced (neuro)inflammation, apoptosis and reduced neurogenesis are associated to the onset of depression." *Progress in Neuro-Psychopharmacology and Biological Psychiatry* 35 (3), 744–59.

Lucassen, P. J., Meerlo, P., Naylor, A. S., van Dam, A. M., Dayer, A. G., Fuchs, E., Oomen, C.A. & Czéh, B. (2010). "Regulation of adult neurogenesis by stress, sleep disruption, exercise and inflammation: Implications for depression and antidepressant action." *European Neuropsychopharmacology* 20 (1), 1–17.

van Praag, H. M. (2004). "Can stress cause depression?" *Progress in Neuro-Psychopharmacology and Biological Psychiatry* 28 (5), 891–907.

Wager-Smith, K. & Markou, A. (2011). "Depression: A repair response to stress-induced neuronal microdamage that can grade into a chronic neuroinflammatory condition?" *Neuroscience & Biobehavioral Reviews* 35 (3), 742–64.

Stress and schizophrenia

Giovanoli, S., Engler, H., Engler, A., Richetto, J., Voget, M., Willi, R., Winter, C., Riva, M. A., Mortensen, P. B., Schedlowski, M. & Meyer, U. (2013). "Stress in puberty unmasks latent neuropathological consequences of prenatal immune activation in mice." *Science* 339 (6123), 1095–99.

Holloway, T., Moreno, J. L., Umali, A., Rayannavar, V., Hodes, G. E., Russo, S. J. & González-Maeso, J. (2013). "Prenatal stress induces schizophrenia-like alterations of serotonin 2A and metabotropic glutamate 2 receptors in the adult offspring: Role of maternal immune system." *Journal of Neuroscience* 33 (3), 1088–98.

Jansen, L. M., Gispen-de Wied, C. C. & Kahn, R. S. (2000). "Selective impairments in the stress response in schizophrenic patients." *Psychopharmacology* 149 (3), 319–25.

Zimmerman, E. C., Bellaire, M., Ewing, S. G. & Grace, A. A. (2013). "Abnormal stress responsivity in a rodent developmental disruption model of schizophrenia." *Neuropsychopharmacology* 23 (3), 223–39.

ANTIDEPRESSANT WITHDRAWAL

Miller, M. C. (2001). "Symptoms that start when an antidepressant stops." *The Harvard Mental Health Letter* (February), 7–8.

Acknowledgments

Knowledge and ideas are good things, but unless they can be communicated to others, they don't go anywhere. I am deeply indebted to the Helpguide.org team, including Lawrence Robinson and Melinda Smith, that supported me throughout the process of writing this book. I am also grateful to Sanjay Nambiar and Beth Davies for their ideas and editing suggestions. In addition, I owe a debt of gratitude to BenBella's publisher, Glen Yeffeth, the design staff, and editors, especially Vy Tran, whose collective skill went into the publication of this book. I have never worked with a team that put more effort and caring into the publishing process.

About the Author

JEANNE SEGAL, PhD, has been helping individuals and families for forty years as a psychologist and emotional intelligence expert. Her books have been published in thirteen languages.

Dr. Segal is an innovator in the fields of holistic health, attachment, emotional intelligence, stress reduction, and relationships. She coordinated a series of conferences linking brain development to the emotional relationship between infants and their caretakers.

Dr. Segal and her husband, Robert, are the founders of Helpguide.org, a nonprofit mental health site focusing on how individuals can empower themselves and bring about life-altering social and emotional change. The site helps over 65 million readers annually.